Where Business Fails

Business Government Relations
at the Federal Level
in Canada

James Gillies

WHERE BUSINESS FAILS

James Gillies

The Institute / L'Institut
for Research on Public Policy / de recherches politiques

Printed in Canada
ISBN 0 920380 53 0

Legal Deposit Fourth Quarter
Bibliothèque nationale du Québec

Canadian Cataloguing in Publication Data
Gillies, James M., 1924-
   Where business fails

Bibliography: p.
ISBN 0-920380-53-0

1. Industry and state — Canada.   I. Institute for
Research on Public Policy.   II. Title.

HD3616.C22G54   322'.3'0971   C82-090001-X

The Institute for Research on Public Policy/L'Institut de recherches politiques
2149 Mackay Street, Montreal, Quebec, H3G 2J2

For the executives, directors,
and officials who provided
the information upon which
this monograph is based.

Table of Contents

Introduction

In the spring of 1980, whether they liked it or not, and most did not, chief executive officers (CEOs) of major Canadian corporations, as CEOs in all enterprise economies, were spending more and more of their time managing relationships with government; and there is every indication that this management activity is going to take even more of their time in the future than it has in the past. Indeed, practitioners and scholars both agree that the great challenges to corporate managers in the next two decades are not going to be found in the traditional management fields — production, marketing, financing, and so on — but rather in relating the firm to the environment within which it operates and in maintaining a role for the private sector in the economy. The former will require new forms of internal corporate organization and new strategies and tactics for working with government; the latter will require demonstration that the public interest is efficiently and effectively served by the operation of a vital private sector.

Dealing with government and the impact of ever-increasing amounts of legislation is not easy under any circumstances, but it was particularly difficult in Canada at the beginning of the 1980s, not only because of the sheer amount of government activity, but also, and perhaps more importantly, because during the 1970s major changes were made in the way the federal government made decisions — and the implications of the changes are not yet fully understood. It is clear, however, that when Mr. Trudeau introduced his collective Cabinet decision-making system in 1968, he set in motion a series of organizational, and therefore power, changes in the Cabinet, the bureaucracy, and to a lesser degree in the legislature, which are still being absorbed, adapted to, and analysed, and which dramatically altered many of the relationships between the governed and the governing that had existed in Canada for decades.

No sector of society has been more affected by the change than business, and no sector has adapted less to it. Traditionally, CEOs and other spokesmen for the private sector have made their impact on the policy-making process of government through contacting senior public servants and ministers; and this type of approach is well understood, well known, and highly regarded in the business community. However, the alteration in the way in which the government makes decisions has meant that the days of the great, in their areas of responsibility and authority almost absolute, power of individual ministers, deputy ministers, and departments is gone; and with a decline in power has come a decline in influence. Consequently, if businessmen wish to have significant impact on the evolution of public policy in the future, they must develop new methods of working with government — the traditional approaches are no longer effective.

This monograph is written for the CEO who is concerned about the evolving role of the corporation in society and the issues created for him, as an executive, by the growth of government. In this context, the changing nature of the decision-making process in government, the ability of government to set and achieve public goals, the need for reform in government institutions, the attitude of CEOs about government and politics, possible alternative approaches to government-business relations, and the mechanisms for dealing with government are examined. The analysis is limited to a study of activities at the federal level of government, although it is very important, in certain cases more important, for corporations to interact effectively with provincial and municipal governments. The significance of, and the techniques for, handling the day-to-day dealings between business and government — tax rulings, tariff changes, interpretation of regulations, and so on, which are so important and so inevitable in a modern economy, are not discussed.

All generalizations are false including the generalization that all generalizations are false. This epigram is never truer than when applied to generalizations about business and the private sector. The degree of difference among firms can best be appreciated by remembering that in 1976 there were about 1,075,000 businesses operating in Canada, of which some 750,000 were unincorporated, and that this unincorporated group included over 430,000 self-employed professionals, farmers, fishermen, and salespersons. In that year, 99 per cent of all business organizations — regardless of form or structure — had sales of less than $2 million and together they accounted for about 28 per cent of all domestic sales. In that same year, the 325,000 incorporated business firms in Canada accounted for almost 90 per cent of business activity.[1]

The characteristics of the owners and managers of various enterprises differ enormously.[2] Indeed, even among businesses of the same size, there are differences depending upon the nature of the product produced or service rendered; and even within the same industries, there are differences among firms because of differences in size. In short, it is difficult, if not impossible, to generalize about "the business community" or "the private sector."

Because of this lack of uniformity, it is impossible to characterize "business's approach" to government in a single, simple manner — what some firms think is appropriate government behaviour, others deplore. Moreover, the complexity of the modern economy and the range of activities of both the government and the corporation often lead to a relationship between a firm and the government that at one and the same time may be adversarial in one area and co-operative in another.[3] It is no wonder that the public is often confused about the relationship between the private and the public sectors.

Although they relate to government in a wide variety of ways, most companies, large or small, producers or sellers, have basically two things in common: they want to remain in private hands and they resist increasing government regulation. In these respects, although not in any clear definition of what they want government to do, private-sector businesses have common cause. While this study focuses on the relationship between large corporations and government, it should be noted that the fundamental goals of small organizations are not significantly different from those of the large — to earn a profit, to survive, and to act in a responsible fashion in the society of which they are a part.

The data upon which much of the analysis is based were provided by the chief executive officers and directors of corporations, trade association managers, elected and non-elected government officials, and students and scholars of government and business. In addition, I have drawn heavily from my own experiences in Ottawa from 1972 to 1980 as a Member of Parliament and Senior Policy Adviser to the Prime Minister. The book is not, however, in any way a personal memoir.

I am deeply indebted to everyone who readily supplied me with their views — they are listed in Appendix A — and to my colleagues both present and former, in Ottawa and at York University.

Through the years I have had the opportunity of discussing the issues raised in this study with literally hundreds of people. I am indebted to all, but I would be remiss if I did not mention Sandford Borins, Jerry Dermer, George Gardiner, D. Horvath, John D. Leitch, I.A. Litvak, Calvin McLaughlin, William Neville, Gordon Robertson, Murray Ross, and Malcolm Taylor, and I thank them for the time they have spent discussing with me the complex relationship between business and the federal government. I also wish to thank Katherine Volesky, research assistant *par excellence* and Donna Cyr for typing the many drafts in exemplary fashion.

I am resigned to the fact that many of my colleagues in the academic community will consider the study distressingly superficial and that my associates and friends in the business community will find it much too academic. Be that as it may, my purpose will be fulfilled if at least some in both groups are sufficiently stimulated to join in the search for new and effective strategies that will eventually lead to less tension and conflict between the public and private sectors in Canada.

James Gillies
Faculty of Administrative Studies
York University, Toronto

Notes

[1] Department of Industry, Trade and Commerce, *Small Business in Canada: A Statistical Profile* (Ottawa: The Department, 1979), p. 1.

[2] There is a perception that small business has received relatively little attention from policy makers, economists, and educational institutions, and has suffered from a benign neglect. See R. Peterson, *Small Business: Building a Balanced Economy* (Erin: Procépic Press, 1977), p. 17. This situation is unquestionably changing primarily because of the work of John Bullock and the Canadian Federation of Independent Business, probably the most successful special interest group operation in Canada.

[3] James E. Post, "The Corporation in the Public Policy Process — A View Toward the 1980s," *Sloan Management Review* 21 (Fall 1979), p. 46.

Government and Business: The Changing Proportions

1

As Canada entered the last two decades of the twentieth century, the interrelationship between business, particularly between the chief executive officers and directors of large corporations, and the federal government was, at best, strained. Whether or not there was a legitimate reason for the tension is another question. Such an astute observer of the political and economic scene as Eric Kierans commented:

> For the life of me, I cannot understand the hostility of the business community to the Trudeau government. It cannot be on the basis of what the federal government has done for, literally, big business has never had it so good. With the exception of the United Kingdom, I doubt that any nation in the world has given its Corporate 1000 a more handsome gift package of subsidies, tax allowances, two-year write-offs, deductibility of merger costs, cheap loans, export credits and insurance than our present Trudeau government. If this be socialism, business should cry for more. . . .[1]

Business management, however, did not see it that way. Indeed, more than half of the respondents to a survey of the readers of the *Business Quarterly* of the School of Business at the University of Western Ontario reported, in the spring of 1979, that the extent of government involvement in their industries was high and they expected it would increase, that over-regulation was a serious problem, that a continuation of current government policies would severely hurt their firms, and that a greater reliance on the market system would help their industries.[2]

Moreover, in 1980 almost half of the CEOs of the largest private corporations believed that the climate for doing business in Canada was going to deteriorate during the first five years of the 1980s, about one third thought it would remain about the same, and the balance thought it would improve.[3]

What a far cry this was from the situation in the immediate post–World War II period when C.D. Howe, Minister of Trade and Commerce, was "in short, the leader of a national business community as well as a party leader and a minister of the crown . . . [who] saw no contradiction in his role; it was his job to enforce the public interest, and the public interest was, ultimately, business's interest."[4] Pleasant, productive, and fruitful as that arrangement was, it is really not astonishing that a quarter of a century later it no longer exists, at least not in anything like the same way. The change in social values in the post-war period led to a questioning of all types of relationships — including that between business and government — and the rejection by many, both within business and government, of the proposition that the public interest was necessarily the interest of business, and vice versa. Moreover, the growth of government activity, in both absolute and relative terms, alone had within it the potentiality — although certainly not the necessity — for increasing conflict and misunderstanding between the private and public sectors.

The Growth of Government

In the future, as has been the case in the past, Canadians will continuously choose whether they want the goods and services that they use produced by the public or the private sector. If they choose the same way in the next two decades as they have in the past three, by the year 2000 more than half of all gross national expenditure in Canada will flow through governments.[5] It is, of course, not inevitable that government activity will increase, but if the past is prologue to the future, it certainly will.

There are a variety of ways of measuring the role of government in the economy. The most common is by estimating the share of gross national product — the value of all goods and services produced in the nation at market prices — flowing through government. In 1980, that proportion was 43 per cent. This does not mean that 43 per cent of all the goods and services produced in the nation were produced by the government, because much of the measured expenditure of government is simply a transfer payment — that is, it records a transfer of income from one group in society to another. For example, family allowance payments flow through the federal government, but the government does not determine how the funds are used by the recipient, and therefore such government activity does not determine what goods and services are produced, or whether they are produced in the private or the public sector.[6] Transfer payments cannot, however, be excluded when assessing the role of the government in the economy for their amount is a factor in determining the total level of expenditures by government, which in turn influences the total level of economic activity in the nation.

For anyone interested in assessing the changing relationship between the public and private sectors, a much more significant indicator is the amount of direct economic activity undertaken by governments. By this measure the growth of the public sector has indeed been prodigious. In the period 1947–1951, only 3.7 per cent of all goods and services produced in Canada were the consequence of direct government activity; by the mid-1970s, the share had increased to 13.9 per cent,[7] and by 1980, it was estimated to be approximately 16.0 per cent. Between 1950 and 1980, the proportion of total gross national expenditure, in real terms attributable to government, increased from 27.0 to 48.0 per cent:[8] there was a 70.0 per cent faster rate of growth in the government's share than there was in total expenditures.[9] Large as that increase is, in the same period direct government activity in the economy increased by 400.0 per cent. While one hears much about the great explosion in government expenditures caused by transfer payments, such spending has not been nearly as significant, in relative terms, in the increase, as has been the phenomenal rate of expansion of the direct role that the government is playing in the economy.

Another measure of the growing role — and probably the one most commonly used — of the federal government in society is simply the change in the amount of federal spending.[10] In 1980, the central government spent over $50 billion — almost 250 per cent more than in 1970. Indeed, during the 1970s, expenditures increased so much faster than revenues that the budget deficit in 1980, alone, was equal to 75 per cent of *all* revenues in 1970.

In addition to financing the traditional functions of government, this vast increase in expenditures was used, among other things, to:

- Increase family allowances and old age pensions
- Inaugurate the Canada Pension Plan
- Initiate the guaranteed income supplement
- Develop a universal programme of hospital and medical care
- Expand and consolidate welfare programmes under the Canada Assistance Plan
- Inaugurate manpower training
- Increase unemployment insurance benefits
- Attempt to reduce regional economic disparities
- Increase support for broadcasting, the arts, humanities, and social sciences
- Extend support to virtually all post-secondary schools
- Institute a large-scale bilingualism programme
- Accept a broader mandate in science and technology, initiating projects in satellite communications and nuclear plants
- Develop programmes of environmental control

- Massively subsidize oil imports
- Establish a national petroleum company
- Aid less-developed nations
- Regulate and co-ordinate foreign investment and some elements of prices and wages
- Market food products, protecting consumers and conserving energy.

And the list is by no means exhaustive.[11]

The administration of this increase in government activity required a concomitant expansion of government structure and employment. When the famous Glassco commission reported on government organization in 1962, there were 34 departments and branches designated as departments under the Financial Administration Act and 337,000 government employees in departments and Crown agencies.[12] Fifteen years later, there were more than 500,000 employees and "the Treasury Board Secretariat published a list of what it described as 'Government-owned and Controlled Corporations'. This added an astounding 310 agencies to the 54 listed Crown corporations and, with the 43 branches designated as departments, brought the total number of Crown agencies to 407. As of January 1979 the official count was 426."[13]

In short, by any definition, the role of the government in Canada increased tremendously in the post-war period. The increase was accompanied, perhaps inevitably, by a shift in the nature of governmental activity from the traditional tasks of building infrastructure to the direct production of goods and services, as well as to the financing of important social services through the massive transfer of funds among governments and individuals. Naturally, all this has been accompanied by a vast increase in the bureaucracies of governments. By 1980, the impact of government on the life of all Canadians in all regions and in all occupations was vastly greater than it had been three decades earlier.

The increase in government activity was not the consequence of any particular plan or scheme on the part of public servants or elected politicians, but rather simply the result of the demands by the public on the government to do more things — and governments responded. Whether this is good or bad is another question, but it is the reality. Accepting and understanding that reality, and the factors that created it, are fundamental for the development of any effective programme of business-government relations.

Why Government Activity
Has Grown

Why did Canadians in the post–World War II period elect governments that increased the proportion of goods and services produced in
the public sector, in relative terms, by four times?

In spite of all that has been written about the relationship between
the public and private sectors, the answer to this question is not to be
found in political theory.[14] Rather, the explanation for the phenomenal
growth of government in Canada lies in geography, history, culture,
and the power of an idea.

Canadians have never been particularly concerned about the direct
intervention of the government in the economy. Indeed, one of the
conditions for the Maritime provinces entering Confederation was the
financing by the state of a railroad to Halifax. Sir John A. Macdonald
used the resources of the nation to assist the construction of the
Canadian Pacific Railroad as a necessary instrument for assuring the
extension of the country from the Atlantic to the Pacific, and in the
twentieth century, the Conservative government of R.B. Bennett had
no ideological difficulties in proposing a state-owned radio network.
The great friend of business in government, C.D. Howe, as a basic
principle of economic development, proposed that there should always
be one large national project — such as a seaway or a pipeline — in
process in Canada. Indeed, the standard interpretations of Canadian
economic history assign the state a major role in guiding and
stimulating growth.[15]

Another significant reason for extensive use of the state, by all
governments since the days of Confederation, has been to protect the
Canadian identity from erosion by the power and force of the United
States. Regardless of any intentions a neighbour may have, the very
presence of a ten-times-larger country on the border creates a
situation whereby collective action to assure the continuation of
culture, economic sovereignty, and identity has often necessitated
state action.

The ready acceptance of a high level of state action is also partially a
legacy of the British in Canada — particularly the British Empire
Loyalists — who brought with them a respect of law, order, and
institutions that placed great emphasis on social stability. This in turn
led to a general collectivist attitude towards society — particularly
among the power élites — which resulted in general support for the
state undertaking activities that under a different political philosophy
would have been left to the individual.[16] In spite of considerable
contention to the contrary, the traditional liberal philosophy, as best
expressed by John Stuart Mill, that the role of the state is simply to
provide a framework within which the private sector can organize the

factors of production and operate without interference, has never been widely held in Canada. The appropriateness of the government taking on activities that the private sector could not or would not do when such activities were perceived to be in the public interest was seldom questioned, and it is reasonable to assume that this basic pragmatic philosophy will continue to be significant, although perhaps less significant than in the past, in determining the evolution of the Canadian economy.

Whether or not one agrees with those who argue that the state has been used so much for collective action that "Canada, in its essentials, is a public enterprise country, always has been, and probably always will be,"[17] one must agree that there is not, and never has been, and probably never will be an enterprise ethic in Canada similar to that of the United States. Consequently, CEOs cannot look to the experience of business in dealing with government in that country with any hope of gaining guidance for dealing with government in Canada.[18]

History, philosophy, and geography may help to explain why there has never been any active resistance to increased government activity in the economy, but they still do not offer a clear reason why Canadians have supported governments that have led to such a large increase in state activity since World War II. Some attribute it to urbanization: the more people are congested the greater the collective services they need. Others suggest technology and innovation have made it possible for governments to do more, and some think it is simply the cumulative result of larger and larger governments — that is, once a bureaucracy reaches a certain size, it has self-perpetuating growth. None of these explanations is persuasive.

If there is one underlying explanation for the greater growth of government in the post-war period, it probably is found more in technical economic theory than anywhere else. Keynes was correct when he wrote that in the long run it is ideas that have consequences, and there is little doubt that the impact of Keynes' theories — and for a period of time their effective implementation — conditioned people in the post-war period into believing that the government was able to perform services that were never assigned to it before.

The essence of Keynes is that government can, through judicious application of monetary and fiscal policies, maintain relatively full employment, hopefully with relatively stable prices. Building on this theory, the first chairman of the Economic Council of Canada, John Deutsch, stated the goals of Canadian economic policy to be the maintenance of full employment, price stability, viability in the balance of payments, less regional disparities in income, and a more equitable distribution of income[19] — goals never assumed by government prior to World War II, and which could only be fulfilled with much more government intervention in the economy.

In addition, economists and politicians throughout the world were influenced during the 1940s by the Beveridge report, which provided a blueprint for a post-war Britain devoid of poverty and want.[20] It was believed by many economists that government could eliminate depressions and solve social problems, and by the mid-1950s, this belief had extended far beyond the academic and government communities to the public at large.

So while introduction of various government programmes was conditioned by a wide range of forces, personalities, and institutions, the fundamental fact that made government intervention possible was the belief by the majority of Canadians — a belief reinforced by the effective way in which the government managed the waging of World War II and the spectacular post–World War II recovery and growth — that the government could solve all problems. As Peter F. Drucker put it, " . . . rarely has there been a more torrid political love affair than that between government and the generations that reached manhood between 1918 and 1960. Anything anyone felt needed doing during this period was to be turned over to the government. . . ."[21] Very simply, because people believed government could solve problems and because government did solve many problems, the people supported politicians who increased the role of government in society.

This is not to say that ideology ruled — that Canadians became Keynesians or, indeed, that even all politicians and officials were Keynesian. Rather, the Keynesian approach was accepted in the post-war period because it worked — and in Canadian government this has always been what mattered. Above everything else in Canadian politics, pragmatism has ruled. There has never been a broad acceptance of any political philosophy: neither Marx and his view that the state should own all resources, nor Mill and the concept of the free competitive market. The state's role has grown simply because the people have believed that the government can do many things — market wheat, produce atomic reactors, provide an outlet for individual Canadians' investment funds, and so forth — better than the private sector. And all in response to perceived problems, not in response to ideology.

Public Sector Expansion: Does It Matter?

If the growth of the role of government in Canadian economic life is a pragmatic response to perceived needs, does it matter that the state plays such a much larger role in the economy? Does it matter if the role of the state grows even more?

The arguments against state intervention are numerous and well known. Some are spurious, all are controversial. Richard Bird argues that there is no reason to think that public-sector activities are automatically unproductive, that a large government is necessarily less productive than a smaller one, or that government expenditures financed by taxes necessarily crowd out private-sector activity (the Eltis argument), and he could be correct.[22] But there are reasons to believe — reasons that are not controversial — that larger and larger government activities are less and less compatible with individual freedom, and in a democratic society, this alone is a compelling reason to question any growth in government in society.[23]

There are two additional specific reasons for concern about the growth in government in Canada. The first is that the increase in government activity has had major structural impacts in the economy — impacts that probably began to be influential during the 1970s when the economy for the first time in the post-war period continuously performed poorly. Indeed, unlike the 1950s and 1960s, the 1970s were characterized by persistent and seemingly irreversible high inflation, high unemployment, net outflow (in certain periods) of direct investment, unfavourable current account deficits in the balance of payments, high foreign indebtedness (the greatest of any country in the world), chronic federal budget deficits, growing national debt, slow and declining rates of real growth, and declining productivity.

Logic makes one wonder whether there is a positive correlation between the increase in government activity and the poor performance of the economy. Presumably there is some, and one economist maintains that "the predictable net impact of . . . [the post-war] . . . major policy developments has been to reduce productivity, to increase recorded unemployment, to raise costs and prices, and to impair our international competitive economic position vis-à-vis the rest of the world."[24]

We cannot draw these conclusions with certainty, however. After all, during the 1970s, dramatic changes occurred in the world economy: the price of energy rose by unprecedented amounts, the international monetary system changed markedly, both the United States and Western Europe suffered high inflation and recession, and the structure of world trade was dramatically influenced by the continued rise in strength of Japan and other Asian countries. Given the fact that over 25 per cent of Canada's economic activity is generated through international trade — Canada has an open economy — the Canadian performance may indeed have been all that could be expected. It can be argued that some of the government's actions that were taken in response to world changes, particularly the cushioning of domestic oil prices, lessened the disruptive impact of international changes on the Canadian economy.

Moreover, it may be hypothesized, indeed it often is, that the problems in the Canadian economy in the 1970s were more a consequence of the private market structure than of increased government activity. While it is recognized that in free markets, under perfectly competitive conditions, output is optimized and adjustments are rapid,[25] no one has ever argued that the Canadian private sector is organized in such a fashion. To the contrary, because of the limited size of the market and the need for economies of scale in production, Canadian firms have larger market shares — there is more concentration — than firms in similar industries in such countries as the United States, West Germany, France, Japan, and Sweden. The lack of the competitive ethic in Canada, which has led to the development of the "mixed economy," has also resulted in an economy where "although Canadian firms are small when compared to the largest firms in the world, they are large relative to the overall size of the Canadian economy or relative to the sizes of individual industries."[26] In fact, the one hundred largest Canadian non-financial corporations had, in 1975, about the same proportion of total domestic sales as the million plus small firms that had sales of less than $2 million annually.[27]

It may be that this concentration of market power led to lower levels of aggregate economic performance in the face of changing world economic conditions than would have been the case if the economy were more competitively organized. If this hypothesis is correct, it is the structure of the private economy, not increased government activity, that led to the poor performance of the economy in 1970. Again, if true, this suggests there should be more government regulation to make the economy more competitive, not less, to improve general economic activity.[28]

Or perhaps there were other factors at work in the 1970s that made it impossible for the economy to fulfil its goals? There were a high number of political uncertainties in the 1970s such as the rise of the Parti Québécois and the changing nature of all federal-provincial relations that were inimical to economic activity. And it has been argued that the high degree of foreign ownership in the economy resulted in Canadian-located, foreign-owned plants bearing more than their fair share of the decline in world trade.

All these conditions may have played a part in causing the poor level of performance, but it does not seem reasonable that a country as rich in resources as Canada — resources in demand throughout the world — should in the 1970s have experienced a decline in real wealth compared to other nations. Moreover, the rise in the federal deficit, the increase in the national debt, the deficits in the balance of payments, the slow growth, and so on, cannot all be a consequence of external factors, market structure, or historical causes. There must be something else at work.

This leads one back to the question of whether or not the great increase in governmental activity has created a situation where the economy in fact is not able to perform as effectively as it did. At any rate, there is sufficient evidence to suggest that any expansion of government activity should not only be assessed in terms of the programme itself but also in terms of the probable impact of such programmes on the economy as a whole. It is far from certain that increased government activity, as the conventional wisdom states, automatically stimulates the economy. Moreover, the view that if the relative size of the public sector, that is, the relationship of government activity to total activity in the economy, remains constant, the absolute size of public-sector activity is irrelevant to the total performance of the economy clearly needs careful examination. In Canada, the point may have been reached where government operations are impairing the capacity of the rest of the economy to perform effectively.[29]

The second specific reason for concern about government growth in Canada is the very legitimate question of whether or not the federal government is able to do for the people what the people want it to do. It is well known that the legislative branch of government, as it now functions, is performing only some of its responsibilities effectively, and there is concern whether or not Parliament can in fact be made viable again. Robert Stanfield has written, "I do not know how the House of Commons can be restored to effective supervision of the government, how we can restore government really responsible to Parliament, except by cutting back on the role of the government,"[30] and "there is, I believe, only one choice. We can accept the loss of parliamentary responsible government or we must accept a more limited role for our federal government."[31] One need not be as pessimistic as Mr. Stanfield about the possibility of reforming Parliament so it can operate more effectively; but one must accept, as a fact, that at the present time the increased role of government in our society, without concomitant reform of Parliament, has led to a situation where by any standards of acceptability, Parliament is not performing adequately.[32]

The breakdown of government is equally apparent in other critical areas. The only truly independent source of information about government spending of public funds is from the Auditor General, and he has reported, "I am deeply concerned that Parliament — and indeed the Government — has lost, or is close to losing, effective control of the public purse. ... financial management and control in the Government of Canada is grossly inadequate. ..."[33] This indictment was repeated in the *Report* of the Royal Commission on Financial Management and Accountability.

The failure of government in its primary task of acting as a trustee of the public's money is well known and has often been decried. What is less well known has been the inability of the government to achieve other important goals. The attempt by the government in the late 1960s and early 1970s to set a series of priorities for the country failed, an effort to establish an industrial strategy for Canada has been unsuccessful, controlling the operations of Crown corporations has not been possible, and establishing a system to limit expenditures has been impossible.

Given the fact that the governments in the 1970s have been unable to complete many well-defined tasks that they set out to do, it is not astonishing that in solving fundamental problems they have been even more unsuccessful. Governments in Canada have not been able to contain inflation, they have not been able to markedly, through their efforts, reduce regional disparities in income, and they have not substantially changed the proportion of the population under the poverty line, despite mammoth expenditures of funds. In fact, with the exception of creating a social welfare system, through redistribution of funds (even in this case much of the cost has been financed by government deficits, which increased dramatically between 1970 and 1980 and these deficits in turn may well have been the single most important factor in creating inflation), the recent failures of government have been greater than its successes.

The fact is, " . . . there is mounting evidence that government is big rather than strong; that it is fat and flabby rather than powerful; that it costs a great deal but does not achieve much. . . ."[34] It is becoming more difficult, even if one rejects the argument that the government has become too large to be effective, to accept uncritically the proposition that increased government activity is always in the public interest. By the beginning of the 1980s, many people were becoming concerned about the growth of government, not for ideological reasons, but simply because experience indicated that government cannot automatically solve all problems.[35]

At any rate, there is sufficient evidence to suggest that the government has become so large that any future programmes need to be considered not only on their own merits but also on their impact on the economy in general.

Will the Role of Government Continue to Expand?

While the characteristic feature of the Canadian economy in the post–World War II period was a rapid increase in the role of government, there was some evidence in the late 1970s that the rate of increase was slowing down. In absolute terms, government activity continued to grow, but relative to the rate of growth in the gross national product, the government's share of growth was declining.

There are various reasons for this, not the least of which was the government's need to relate government expenditures more closely to revenues, but probably the most important was that over the preceding three decades, the foundations of the welfare state had been put in place in Canada. Universal old age pensions, unemployment insurance, national medical and hospital care, and children's allowances have become part of the fabric of Canadian society. These programmes may be modified and additional ones added, but by and large the social welfare revolution is complete and with it the rapid rate of increase in the transfer of funds through government from one sector of society to another.

The major economic issues facing the government in the final decades of the twentieth century will centre around bringing inflation under control, providing real growth, assuring full employment, and lessening regional disparities of income. The fundamental question is, how will these goals — this fulfilment of the public interest — be achieved? Since both the private sector and the government have the same goal — a prosperous economy, one might conclude that the role of the state in the economy might well decline in the future. But this may not happen for two reasons. First, many CEOs believe, perhaps incorrectly, that the manner in which the economy was managed by the government throughout most of the 1970s has created an environment within which it is impossible for corporations to operate at anything close to their maximum potential. They point out that although Canada had in place in 1980 one of the most attractive tax systems in the Western world for encouraging investment in plant and equipment, such investment was low, relative to need, and productivity declined. Given the high levels of inflation, which many believe were generated primarily because of government's inability to manage its own finances — the federal deficit in 1980 was the highest both in absolute terms and relative to the budget in any peace-time year — plus what they perceive as undue regulations and an anti-business basis, they are not confident that the private sector can be as effective as an instrument for growth in the future as it was in the past.

Second, at the very time when the private sector, because of the economic environment, appears to be less effective in providing high levels of economic activity, the policies used by governments since the end of World War II to maintain high levels of economic activity and relative stability of prices — primarily macroeconomic policies — are becoming ineffective. Indeed, there is considerable question as to whether or not the traditional Keynesian approach can work in the environment of government deficits that characterizes the economy in the 1980s.

Given the fact that both the private and public sectors are operating inefficiently — and both to some degree for the same reason — the government could withdraw from many of its activities and concentrate on getting government spending under control, in order that both private and public policies could once again operate effectively.

Or it could take another approach. If there are continuing levels of high unemployment and the broad levers of policy formulation — changing revenue and expenditure patterns to stimulate consumption and investment — do not bring effective results, then the government may well decide to intervene more directly to provide jobs. For example, to assure employment, it could support directly, through loans and equity, corporations that have financial troubles, regardless of how inefficient their operations may be. It could create new enterprises or take over existing firms.

Moreover, there is no reason to suppose that they would not operate in such a fashion. Governments in Canada are not, and never have been, constrained by either philosophical or ideological reasons from taking direct action in the economy when they perceive it in the public interest to do so. An example of this type of response to perceived problems has been the movement of the federal government into the energy field through the establishment of a national oil company — and there is no evidence to indicate the public does not support such a move; on the contrary, they widely support the action. Governments have also taken over all or part of two other major resource industries — potash in Saskatchewan and asbestos in Quebec — and in the 1970s the government of Alberta purchased an airline.

The irony of the situation for management in the private sector is that the very conditions that may have made the private sector less effective and that therefore provide the rationalization for more government intervention will be exacerbated by such policies. Ever more government intervention in the economy may make the private sector even less efficient, and less efficiency in the private sector will be justification for more government intervention.

Consequently, despite the congruence between the public- and the private-sector interests and the concern by many that government is not capable of solving many of the nation's problems, there could well be more involvement by government in the economy in the future than has been characteristic of the Canadian society in the past. It may well be that the position of various firms and industries as the fundamental instruments for organizing the production of goods and services in the economy will be extensively challenged.

The implications of the possibility of such developments for CEOs is clear. At the very least, companies must organize their management processes in such a manner that the consequences of rapid political and social change are understood when decisions are made, and the

CEO will have to be more aware of his responsibility of assuring the continuing operation of the enterprise for his shareholders.

But there is another implication for CEOs that is equally significant and much more difficult. They must decide what their obligations are in defining and determining how the public interest should be fulfilled. If they believe, as many do, that the highest standard of living for the most Canadians can be achieved through the efficient operation of the private sector, then they must determine how they can make the greatest contribution towards fulfilling the public interest. If in their opinion the public interest is served through less government activity in the economy, not more, what can and should they do? More fundamentally, can they do anything that is effective? The answer clearly depends upon the manner in which the public interest is determined in a democratic society, and the legitimacy of the corporation, both perceived and real, in the Canadian economy.

Notes

[1] Eric Kierans, "The Corporate Challenge to Government," *The Walter L. Gordon Lecture Series 1976–77: The Role of Government in Canadian Society* (Toronto: The Canada Studies Foundation, 1977), p. 22.

[2] Donald H. Thain and Mark Baetz, "Increasing Trouble Ahead for Business-Government Relations in Canada?" *Business Quarterly* 44 (Summer 1979): 56–65.

[3] For details of the CEO and Director survey, see Appendix A.

[4] Robert Bothwell and William Kilbourn, *C.D. Howe: A Biography* (Toronto: McClelland and Stewart, 1979), p. 262.

[5] The actual figure would be approximately 53 per cent. In 1950, government expenditures were 27 per cent of GNE; in 1980, about 42 per cent — displaying the same rate of increase in twenty years, the figure will be 53 per cent.

[6] Grant L. Reuber, *Canada's Political Economy: Current Issues* (Toronto: McGraw-Hill Ryerson, 1980), p. 47.

[7] Richard M. Bird with M.W. Bucovestsky and D.K. Foot, *The Growth of Public Employment in Canada* (Montreal: The Institute for Research on Public Policy, 1979), p. 23.

[8] *Ibid.*, p. 9.

[9] *Ibid.*

[10] In spite of a strong public impression to the contrary, not all the increase in government expenditure took place at the federal level. In fact, when transfer payments are excluded, the federal increase from 11.5 per cent of gross national expenditures in 1950 to 16.1 per cent in 1977 was far outdistanced by the more than doubling of the share of the GNE spent by the provinces — from 5.7 per cent in 1950 to 12.4 per cent in 1977. The percentage increase of expenditures by municipalities was also greater than that of the federal government. See Bird, *op. cit.*, p. 16.

[11] Royal Commission on Financial Management and Accountability, *Progress Report* (Ottawa: Minister of Supply and Services Canada, 1977), pp. 16–17.

[12] Strangely enough, measuring the total amount of public employment is not easy. First, what is public-sector employment? Is a doctor who receives a portion of his income from programmes financed by the taxpayer included? Secondly, there are three sources of

information about such employment — taxation, census, and civil service data — and the information from each is hard to reconcile. About one in four Canadians is employed in the public sector, and this proportion does not seem to have changed dramatically over the past decade, although the share of the public-sector employment in the federal civil service is increasing. For the most complete discussion and analysis of public employment, see Bird, *op. cit.*, p. 36.

13 Royal Commission on Financial Management and Accountability, *Final Report* (Ottawa: Minister of Supply and Services Canada, 1979), p. 277.

14 Bird, *op. cit.*, p. 152; and Michael Pitfield, "The Shape of Government in the 1980s: Techniques and Instruments for Policy Formulation at the Federal Level," *Canadian Public Administration* 19 (Spring 1976), p. 9.

15 H.G.J. Aitken, "Defensive Expansion: The State and Economic Growth in Canada," in *Approaches to Canadian Economic History*, edited by W.T. Easterbrook and M.H. Watkins (Toronto: McClelland and Stewart, 1967), p. 184.

16 Robert Presthus, "Evolution and Canadian Political Culture: The Politics of Accommodation," paper prepared for the *Bi-Centennial Conference on Revolution and Evolution: The Impact of the Revolutionary Experience of the United States Compared with the Development of Canada Solely by Evolution* (North Carolina: Duke University, Canadian Studies Center, 1976).

Presthus argues that the "British legacy had mixed consequences. Among its positive ones is surely a pervasive respect for law and order, which on the whole ensured more social stability than found in the United States. Reinforcing this advantage is an organic political philosophy, manifest in a collectivist attitude toward society, contrasting sharply with the competitive individualism of American life . . .," p. 7, and "compared with the United States, which has . . . had a laissez-faire rationale, ideological support for this condition [i.e., pervasive reliance upon government for support in institutional sectors] is dramatically higher among Canadians political elites . . .," p. 12.

17 Herschel Hardin, *A Nation Unaware: The Canadian Economic Culture* (Vancouver: J.J. Douglas, 1974), p. 140.

18 Given the fact that a large number of Canadian corporate executives have been educated in business schools in the United States and are greatly influenced by management developments in that country, the need for a unique management approach to business-government relations in Canada may be overlooked, and this would be a serious mistake. The political and social environment within which business operates in Canada is fundamentally different from that of the United States — not primarily because of the different forms of government, but because of different philosophical and political attitudes about government. While Canadian business executives have learned much about marketing, finance, production, and general management from the American experience, they cannot expect to learn much about business-government relations from the American business community. For an example of this, see Herbert E. Meyer, "Business Wins One in Canada," *Fortune* (3 July 1978): 84–85. In this assessment of the *Report* of the Royal Commission on Corporate Concentration, the conclusion is reached that the role of the Canadian corporation in the Canadian economy is secure — that government regulation and intervention is not necessarily a growing concern for Canadian business. Such a conclusion could be drawn from the *Report* only when it is evaluated outside the context of Canadian economic, social, and political history. More firms proportionately and absolutely need to be concerned about nationalization in Canada than in the United States, and the *Report* is essentially irrelevant to the question of business survival. In no important respect did the *Report* mean "that business wins one in Canada."

19 Economic Council of Canada, *First Annual Review: Economic Goals for Canada to 1970* (Ottawa: Queen's Printer, 1964). The goals were actually embedded in the legislation establishing the Economic Council of Canada.

20 William H. Beveridge, *Full Employment in a Free Society* (New York: W.W. Norton, 1945).

[21] Peter F. Drucker, *The Age of Discontinuity* (New York: Harper & Row, 1969), p. 213.

[22] Bird, *op. cit.*, p. 125.

[23] See Frederick A. Hayek, *The Road to Serfdom* (Chicago: University of Chicago Press, 1944); and for a contemporary statement, William E. Simon, *A Time for Truth* (New York: McGraw-Hill, 1978).

[24] Reuber, *op. cit.*, p. 44.

[25] George J. Stigler, *Production and Distribution Theories* (New York: Macmillan, 1941), pp. 320–87.

[26] Royal Commission on Corporate Concentration, *Report* (Ottawa: Minister of Supply and Services Canada, 1978), p. 12.

[27] *Ibid.*, p. 21; and Department of Industry, Trade and Commerce, *Small Business in Canada: A Statistical Profile* (Ottawa: The Department, 1979), p. 1.

[28] The fact that there appears to have been relatively little change in corporate concentration over the years indicates that the problems of the 1970s were not a consequence of the form of market organization in Canada. Concentration was approximately the same in 1950 and early 1960 when the economy was operating much closer to its potential. This is not to say, however, that greater competition might not lead to more efficient utilization of resources.

[29] There is a great penchant, particularly on the part of politicians and academicians, to relate the change in the public sector to changes in total activity in the economy. Perhaps this relative measuring has some advantage, but it implicitly implies that as long as the ratio remains the same, the absolute size of government is not significant. Such reasoning rejects the concept of economies of scale; that is, perhaps government does not have to grow as fast as the economy (or perhaps it has to grow faster) to provide the services that people want from government, but much more significantly, such aggregative reasoning avoids the fundamental question of whether or not the taxpayers are receiving the most efficient delivery of services possible for their tax dollar. Government has no intrinsic function of its own. It is the instrument through which people collectively purchase services, and it is the responsibility of the officials of government to provide such services as efficiently as possible. That the share of the gross national expenditures of the nation disbursed by governments is growing at the same, slower or faster rate than the total level of gross national expenditures throws no light on this all-important issue.

[30] Robert L. Stanfield, "The Present State of the Legislative Process in Canada: Myths and Realities," in *The Legislative Process in Canada: The Need for Reform*, edited by W.A.W. Neilson and J.C. MacPherson (Montreal: The Institute for Research on Public Policy, 1978), p. 44.

[31] *Ibid.*, p. 47.

[32] Royal Commission on Financial Management and Accountability, *Final Report*, *op. cit.*, p. 372.

[33] *Report of the Auditor General of Canada to the House of Commons for the Fiscal Year Ended March 31, 1976* (Ottawa: Minister of Supply and Services Canada, 1976), p. 9.

[34] Drucker, *op. cit.*, p. 212.

[35] The failure of government to solve problems is not unique to Canada. In the United States, in spite of a veritable "war on poverty," little progress has been made in eliminating poverty in Appalachia. After billions of dollars of expenditure, the problems of the urban areas were as bad in 1980 as in 1970, and the American economy during the 1970s operated at less than optimum levels. New York City had literally to be salvaged from bankruptcy, and the tragedy of the government management of the war in Viet Nam is well known.

The Corporation and the Public Purpose

2

In a modern democratic state, does the corporation have the right and responsibility of helping to determine the public interest? Moreover, if it does, has the change in the value system of society over the past two decades been such that it is impossible for corporations to fulfil their responsibilities effectively? An assessment of these two questions must underlie the development of any programme for improving the relationship between government and business in Canada.

Modern democracies are based on the consent doctrine of Locke, Rousseau, and Jefferson. This doctrine simply says that those who govern do so with the consent of the governed and whenever the governors enact legislation or perform acts that the majority of the governed disapprove of, they have the right to change those who govern them. The *quid pro quo* between the governing and the governed is that those who are governed have the right, and indeed the responsibility, of making an input into the governing process, of helping to establish the public purpose, and this is done through the political process. Indeed, the fundamental function of the political process, through government, is to work out "through an endless series of compromises, the conflicting interests of those subject to its authority in such a way as to avoid the use of force."[1] In a well-functioning pluralistic society, the interests of all parties are taken into consideration when policy is being determined; and the extent to which some sectors have more influence than others is a measure of the degree to which the system does, or does not, work well. If any great imbalance in power occurs over any long period of time, the system does not survive.

Leaders of the business community should not expect to be able to define the public interest with respect to business — it will be determined through the political process; and they should certainly not expect that the end result of the interplay among groups with competing goals will be policies that have no other purpose than the maximization of profits by the corporation or, indeed, that corporations have no other function than the maximization of profits.[2] At the same time, however, the voluntary acceptance by business of the authority of the state to determine some of the corporations' goals and responsibilities gives the corporation the right, indeed, the responsibility, of helping in determining the goals and responsibilities of the state. As L. Silk and D. Vogel put it, "if . . . businessmen acknowledge that the public has the right to seek to influence, guide, or control the corporation through the political process, as well as in the marketplace, then business may appropriately play an active role in influencing the political values and choices of the community."[3] The community must grant the corporations the right to participate in the determination of the public interest, and most significantly the corporations must accept their responsibility for participating in the public policy formulation process.

There can be, therefore, no question about the propriety, and indeed the necessity, of the corporation playing a role in the determination of the public purpose. But having the right and having an impact are two different things. Certainly, while not a sufficient condition, a necessary one for having any influence is public credibility, and credibility to institutions is not automatically provided by society. Moreover, credibility is normally only granted when it is perceived that the goals of an institution — in this case, the corporation — are reasonably close to the goals of society. In short, it has long been argued by commentators on business-government relations that the corporation can have little impact on public policy — and therefore can do little to influence the forces of government impacting on the corporation — if the public believes that the goals of society and the goals of the corporation are quite different.[4]

In Canada, from Confederation until after World War II, the goals of society and the corporation have been perceived to be much the same. Everyone wanted more output of goods and services and the corporation was the effective instrument through which society could achieve its principal goals of growth.[5] Consequently, until the 1960s there was relatively little criticism of corporations; there was a congruence between the public and the private interest.

The most serious attacks on Canadian corporate activity arise from the belief by some that there is excessive concentration of power in a few corporate hands.[6] And the critics have had some cause for concern. Corporate concentration in Canada is high — much higher than in most industrial countries. Moreover, there has been no consistent effort to limit corporate concentration because the small size of the Canadian market does not permit the economics of scale in production without concentration. The net result has been continuous questioning by Canadians of whether or not in their pluralistic society business interests have been able, because of their relative size and power, to exercise undue influence in the formulation of public policy.

This concern was reflected as recently as 1975 when the government, upon learning of a possible take-over of the Argus Corporation of Toronto by Power Corporation of Montreal, appointed the Royal Commission on Corporate Concentration to examine whether or not there was too much power in the hands of too few businessmen. The commission reported in 1978 that it found little or no evidence of undue influence by corporations on government in the area of policy formulation.[7] But still the perception persists that corporations may have too much power, and for the maintenance of the legitimacy of the private sector it has always been imperative that CEOs demonstrate that corporate size and concentration in Canada are in harmony with the public interest, that they are essential for a prosperous, functioning Canadian economy. For the most part Canadian managers have done this well, and so the concern that Canadians have felt about the size and power of corporations, while real, has never been sufficiently great to cause a general rejection of the legitimacy of the corporation in the economic process.

This perception of congruence was reinforced during World War II when the government, working with the private sector, mobilized resources in a highly effective manner. The growth of affluence in the later post-war period confirmed the view that the enterprise system was capable of providing Canadians with a high standard of living. Consequently, in the 1950s and early 1960s, there was a general harmony between business and the values of society: management concentrated on its central task of producing goods and services and society believed that it was performing a necessary, useful, productive job.

Increasing Affluence and Changing Values

By the mid-1960s, partially as a product of the very affluence that business helped to create, the value system of society began to change. Economic growth for its own sake was questioned. People found themselves living in societies, in Galbraith's phrase, "rich in private goods but poor in public." If, as some contended, "environmental pollution, fluctuations in economic activity, inflation, monopolistic practices, 'manipulation' of the consumer through artificial obsolescence, blatant advertising, incomplete disclosure and low-quality after-sale service"[8] were the price of the free enterprise systems and continuous economic growth, for many the price was too high. By the late 1960s and the early 1970s, a better educated, more prosperous, highly urban population with more leisure and more information was willing to trade more growth for cleaner rivers, fresher air, and less polluted environments. When everyone has a boat, clean rivers become a high priority.

For corporations, the final end product of its success in the 1950s and 1960s was, ironically, that they were forced to operate in an ever-more regulated and restricted environment, and yet they were expected to produce at the same level of efficiency the goods and services that society wanted at about the same cost. Moreover, by the late 1970s, there was a substantial and influential body of opinion that believed that "the sense of identity between the self-interest of the corporation and the public interest had been replaced by a sense of incongruence."[9] Professor Galbraith of Harvard University took the position even further; he contended that as a society became more affluent and the corporation more powerful, power passed from the consumer to the producer, that is, that consumer sovereignty was dead. Since the producer could produce what he wanted, and produced those things that maximized profits, regardless of their consequences to society, there would always be, according to Galbraith, a broad divergence between the interests of producers and the public. The policy implications of Galbraith's analysis — at least for Galbraith — were that the nationalization of the means of production in what he characterized as the "non-market" part of the economy was essential to achieve public goals. For Galbraith, the large corporation ceased to have legitimacy in the 1970s.[10]

Affluence also led to changes in other individual values, which led to additional attacks on the legitimacy of the corporation — not only because it was the instrument of growth, but because of its very form and structure. These have been characterized by D. Yankelovich as a decline in the work ethic, a decline in authority and acceptance of restraint, new attitudes about morality including new attitudes about property, a rise in the wish for immediate self-gratification, acceptance of the concept of entitlement (that is, that people have an automatic right to housing, education, and so on), and a greater stress on harmony with nature.[11]

Every one of these changes in values impacted on the corporation. The decline in the work ethic meant that not everyone accepted hard work as the central means of personal fulfilment; a decline in authority created the need for new management styles and a rise in the elusive concept of participatory democracy; new attitudes about morality, particularly about war, led to criticism of organizations, including business organizations, that contributed to a war effort (Dow Chemical was attacked by students for producing napalm); new attitudes about property meant a decline in the acceptance of the legitimacy of private property; the need for immediate self-gratification meant unwillingness to accept training as a condition for advancement; a rise in the concept of entitlement undermined the belief in personal property rights; and a new interest in being in harmony with nature resulted in increased attention on the environment and the fixing of blame on those perceived to pollute water, and natural beauty. All these together, plus the affluence to afford such views, created a new environment within which both management and government had to operate.

The reaction of governments to the new set of values and concern about corporations was an attempt to protect the public interest through legislation. And there was political support for such action as the corporation came under more and more attack. While criticism in Canada was less virulent than in the United States — there was no native Ralph Nader — there is no question "that issues such as the accountability of corporations, fears of undue corporate power, and a general unease about institutional bigness" were greater in the 1970s than at any time since the 1930s.[12] A less temperate view of the consequences for business of the changing value system was that "the attack on business by antagonistic political interest groups has escalated. . . . consumers, environmentalists, socialists, nationalists, minority language and racial groups, local and regional communities, farmers, women, native peoples, educational and religious factions, and so on . . . [have] the common denominator that they have declared war on business."[13] While this may be an overstatement, there was clearly enough change in public opinion to create great corporate concern.

The reaction of many corporate managers to the same values that were leading to more government legislation and regulation was to alter corporate practices to bring them more in line with the perceived public interest. But was this the proper approach to take? Some practitioners and scholars said yes, some said no, and so began the great Canadian debate on the question of the social responsibilities of the corporation.

Social Responsibilities and the Public Interest

What are the responsibilities of the modern corporation in society? That they have some is clear from their origin. After all, the corporation is the creature of the state and therefore has obligations to it. This relationship has always been recognized. Indeed, in 1858, that great defender of liberty and enemy of the too powerful state, John Stuart Mill, wrote that "trade is a social act. Whoever undertakes to sell any description of goods to the public, does what affects the interest of other persons, and of society in general and thus his conduct, in principle, comes within the jurisdiction of society."[14] The state, without question, has a legitimate right to specify certain things that the corporation must, and must not, do. And some would argue that the legal responsibilities — obeying the law — are all that a corporation, like an individual, should be expected to do. Indeed, to do more, according to commentators such as Milton Friedman, the most widely known opponent of the firm accepting responsibilities beyond those mandated by law, is clearly wrong. Friedman argues:

> In a free-enterprise, private property system, a corporate executive is an employee of the owners of the business. He has direct responsibility to his employers. The responsibility is to conduct the business in accordance with their desires, which generally will be to make as much money as possible while conforming to the basic rules of the society, both those embodied in law and those embodied in ethical custom . . . insofar as his actions in accord with his 'social responsibility' reduce returns to stockholders, he is spending their money . . . "there is one and only one social responsibility of business — to use its resources and engage in activities designed to increase its profits so long as it stays within the rules of the game."[15]

In short, according to Friedman, "few trends could so thoroughly undermine the very foundations of our free society as the acceptance by corporate officials of a social responsibility other than to make as much money for their stockholders as possible."[16]

While Friedman's position underlies all the arguments against corporate managers accepting social responsibilities, the position is also supported on the grounds that accepting such responsibilities makes the price of the product of the firm non-competitive with the products of other non-responsive firms, reduces competitiveness in foreign markets, and detracts from the principal responsibility of the manager. Moreover, it is contended that firms fulfil social obligations poorly; business is not accountable to the public and yet it is the public who are reponsible for choosing, through their elected representatives, the social issues that should be dealt with; and it is not perceived by the public as the task or responsibility of the corporation to deal beyond the requirements of law with social issues, and so there is little public support for such action.

Even some of the leading critics of the corporation argue that business should not get involved in social issues because "current social crises have moral, legal, and political dimensions which only incidentally (if at all) require business skills [for their solution]. . . . Business leaders are inevitably isolated from reality . . . [and] . . . the structure of the corporate system does not provide practical standards upon which the social performance of corporate managers can be judged. . . ."[17]

Opposing the proponents of the "legal requirements view" are those who believe that it is the firm's obligation to evaluate in its decision-making process the effects of its decisions on the external social system in a manner that will accomplish social benefits along with the traditional economic gains that a firm seeks.[18]

The arguments in favour of social responsibility rest on the propositions that such actions improve the public image of the firm, help avoid government regulation, are a simple response to what society wants, allow managers to use their knowledge to help solve social issues, are essential if the private sector is to survive and, most significantly, are the ethical and appropriate way for any institution in society to perform.

Regardless of the merits of the position, there is little doubt that contemporary managers have rejected Friedman's view and have accepted as part of their management mandate the need to direct their corporation in a socially acceptable way — in a manner beyond fulfilling their responsibilities under the law. Some firms, for example, not only have legal charters but also social charters. Leading business organizations such as the Conference Board and the Chamber of Commerce promulgate the idea that business must accept and meet its social responsibilities.

In Canada, the debate about the need of the corporation to accept some social responsibilities is over. As the *Report* of the Royal Commission on Corporate Concentration states, "society expects business to be humane as well as efficient."[19] The public expects more than goods and services from the contemporary corporation. It is widely held that "business exists to serve not only the economic needs of its shareholders, customers and employees, but also the wider economic and social needs of the society in which it operates."[20]

While the public may expect such action on the part of the Canadian corporation, have corporations met the public's expectations?

The simple answer to that question is that no one knows for sure. The Royal Commission on Corporate Concentration had a special study made on the subject and it concluded that (1) the level of involvement in social issues increases with firm size; (2) the greater the profitability of the firm the greater the involvement; (3) the difference with respect to awareness and concern about social issues between Canadian and non-Canadian-owned firms is slight; (4) the involvement varies substantially among industries; and (5) the amount of resources committed to the protection of the physical environment was greater than the amount required by law in all sectors.[21] Even with the results of this analysis, the commissioners reported that assessing the social issues surrounding corporate operations was by far the most difficult part of their mandate.[22]

If the commission, which presumably conducted the most definite study of the corporation recently completed in Canada, comes to any conclusion at all, it is that the Canadian people ought not to expect the corporation to be deeply involved in social issues because "resources are not unlimited; the necessity to make choices means that some wants will be unsatisfied, some desires unfulfilled. The business managers' concern with the monetary and other costs of social responsibility may well be excessive at times, but that attitude can bring a healthy and necessary measure of discipline into the choices that society makes."[23] More specifically, the commission believes that Canadians particularly should not expect much involvement in social issues by corporations engaged in foreign trade — this includes many of the largest — because they must compete with other companies in other countries operating under different circumstances. In short, "to an important extent, the Canadian economy will be only as responsive to social demands as others outside the country will allow it to be."[24] The entire analysis of corporate social responsibility is based on economic considerations, narrowly defined. I find such analysis something less than compelling.

One is inclined to suspect, although it cannot be proven or documented, that until we have better methodology, more information, and agreement by everyone as to what is meant by social responsibility,[25] the level of corporate social responsibility accepted by CEOs is greater in principle than in fact. In the United States, according to one critic, "the conclusion seems irresistible that the reputation of big business as social benefactor is self-made and unfulfilled."[26]

Be that as it may, CEOs have accepted a broader definition of the appropriate role of the corporation in society; they are aware of the change in the public's perception, although they may not always have acted upon it. Moreover, it is very clear that the acceptance of the broader definition of the responsibilities of the corporation has not led to less intervention by the government in the activities of firms or in the economy as a whole. The amount of regulation and government activity has increased at the very time corporations were apparently accepting a higher degree of social responsibility. Whether or not there would have been less government intervention if corporations had done more in terms of social activities is a non-testable hypothesis, but the reality remains that accepting social responsibilities and a broader definition of the role of the corporation in society has not led, as many argued that it would, to less contact, for good or bad, between business and government.

Business-Government Relations: The New Realities

The change in the value system of society in the past decades had led to a change in the environment within which business carries on its dealings with government. Consequently, when developing strategies for working with governments, CEOs must be aware that the political and social climates have changed dramatically since the 1950s and 1960s, and as a consequence:

- Corporations are no longer immune to attack from various elements in society, including governments, because they are effective producers of goods and services, although this is still the fundamental basis of their legitimacy.[27] While the public may express concern and the government may legislate to regulate and correct perceived problems arising from corporate behaviour, it is taken for granted that corporations will continue to do what they are formed to do, that is, produce products in an efficient and effective fashion.

- Business must accept responsibility for the impact of their activity on the various constituencies that they influence — customers, employees, environment, and the national economy. And they must try to keep that impact in reasonable harmony with the public interest. To the extent that they do not do so voluntarily, they will be compelled to do so by law.

- Corporations are never granted credibility and legitimacy when it is perceived that their goals and the public interest are different — since the 1960s credibility is not automatically granted to any organization.

- The public interest changes rapidly and, as it does, the public's view of the proper role of the corporation in the modern state also changes. One should not make the mistake of believing that the decline in influence of critics such as Ralph Nader at the end of the 1970s marked the start of a period when management had to be less concerned about attacks on the corporation. Rather, Nader's influence dropped because the public's concern moved from social issues to economic problems — issues in which Nader did not play a dominant role.

All this means that if the corporation is to have a significant role in the economy in the future, its place in society must be defended and promoted. Fulfilling this responsibility may well become one of the most important tasks of the CEOs in the years ahead.

Notes

[1] Douglas G. Hartle, *Public Policy Decision Making and Regulation* (Montreal: The Institute for Research on Public Policy, 1979), p. 34.

[2] Leonard Silk and David Vogel, *Ethics and Profits: The Crisis of Confidence in American Business* (New York: Simon and Schuster, 1978), p. 146.

[3] *Ibid.*, p. 158.

[4] James E. Post, "The Corporation in the Public Policy Process — A View Toward the 1980s," *Sloan Management Review* 21 (Fall 1979), p. 50.

[5] Daniel Bell, "The Corporation and Society in the 1970's," *The Public Interest* (Summer 1971), pp. 5–13.

[6] The major difference between Canada and the United States is that the attacks on the corporation that coalesced around the populous movement in western Canada in the

Depression eventually ended up in the formation of the C.C.F. party — now the N.D.P., a viable socialist political force — which rejects the corporate form as the optimum organization for the production of goods and services. There is no strong socialist party in the United States.

7   Royal Commission on Corporate Concentration, *Report* (Ottawa: Minister of Supply and Services, Canada, 1978), p. 410.

8   H. Igor Ansoff, "The Changing Shape of the Strategic Problem," in *Strategic Management: A New View of Business Policy and Planning*, edited by Dan E. Schendel and Charles W. Hofer (Boston: Little, Brown, 1979), p. 34.

9   Bell, *op. cit.*, p. 7.

10 This is a highly truncated version of the Galbraith argument, but not of his conclusions. See J. K. Galbraith, *Economics and the Public Purpose* (Boston: Houghton, Mifflin, 1973). Unfortunately for Galbraith's argument, much of its empirical support is drawn from the automobile industry, which Galbraith contends is able to control what the consumer buys. Clearly he did not foresee the reality of the United States' automobile market of the early 1980s, or he could never have drawn such conclusions.

11 I.D. Yankelovich, "Social Values," in the William Elliot Lectures as quoted in M.D. Richards, *Organizational Goal Structures* (St. Paul: West Publishing, 1978), pp. 71–72.

12 Royal Commission on Corporate Concentration, *op. cit.*, p. 373.

13 Donald H. Thain, "The Mistakes of Business in Dealing with Politics and Government," *Business Quarterly* 44 (Autumn, 1979), p. 46.

14 John Stuart Mill, "On Liberty," in *Utilitarianism, Liberty, and Representative Government* (New York: E.P. Dutton, 1951), p. 202.

15 Milton Friedman, "The Social Responsibility of Business Is to Increase Its Profits," *The New York Times Magazine* (13 September 1970).

16 Milton Friedman, *Capitalism and Freedom* (Chicago: University of Chicago Press, 1962), p. 133.

17 Joel F. Henning, "Corporate Social Responsibility: Shell Game for the Seventies?" in *Corporate Power in America*, edited by Ralph Nader and Mark J. Green (New York: Grossman, 1973), pp. 157–59.

18 Keith Davis and Robert L. Blomstron, *Business, Society, and Environment: Social Power and Social Response*, 2d ed. (New York: McGraw-Hill, 1971), p. 85.

19 Royal Commission on Corporate Concentration, *op. cit.*, p. 380.

20 *Ibid.*, pp. 376–77.

21 R. Terrance Mactaggart, Donald Kelly, Peter Broadmore, and Lee E. Preston, *Corporate Social Performance in Canada*, study prepared for the Royal Commission on Corporate Concentration (Ottawa: Minister of Supply and Services Canada, 1977), pp. 23–65. The survey is supplemented by case studies of nine major corporations, but one reviewer suggests that their usefulness is extremely limited because they are simply statements of what individual firms say is their policy concerning social issues. No attempt is made to test whether the policies are implemented and, if implemented, whether they are effective. See R. Schwindt, "Business and Society: A Review of the Work of the Royal Commission," in *Perspectives on the Royal Commission on Corporate Concentration*, edited by Paul Gorecki and W.T. Stanbury (Montreal: The Institute for Research on Public Policy, 1979), p. 294.

22 Royal Commission on Corporate Concentration, *op. cit.*, p. 373.

23 *Ibid.*, p. 381.

[24] *Ibid.*

[25] The reality is that in spite of literally hundreds of speeches, debates, and articles, there has not been a great deal of improvement in the definition of "social responsibilities" since 1953, when Bowen wrote "that corporations should do those things that are desirable in terms of the objectives and values of society," and since those values and objectives change through time, the social responsibilities of corporations change with them.

[26] Henning, *op. cit.*, p. 157.

[27] It is interesting to note that while the large oil companies for years were under criticism for contributing to pollution, following monopoly practices, and exercising excessive power, it was not until the companies could not supply the gasoline that people wanted — particularly in the United States where people had to line up at the pumps and gas rationing was a very real possibility — that the fundamental legitimacy of the private energy companies was seriously questioned.

The Chief Executive Officer and the Determination of the Public Interest

3

In the summer of 1980, almost half of the CEOs of Canada's largest corporations believed that the climate for doing business in Canada would deteriorate during the first half of the 1980s, about one third thought that it would remain the same, and the balance — about 17 per cent — believed that it would improve.[1]

It would be easy to ascribe this pessimism to the simple fact that the role of the government in society has been increasing rapidly, which in itself has increased the interface between business and government, and more contact often means more conflict. Moreover, one might assume that businessmen automatically object to a larger degree of activity by government; but this is not necessarily so, for through most of Canada's history the government and the business community have worked closely together to fulfil the public interest. In the early post–World War II period, even when the role of the government in the economy was rapidly expanding, there was a high degree of confidence by the public and private sectors in each other. Indeed, the relationship between ministers of the Crown such as C.D. Howe and Robert Winters and senior Canadian business executives was very close.

The fact that the role of government in society has increased is not, therefore, a sufficient explanation for the growing conflict between the private and public sectors. Many other forces are at play, and it is only through an understanding of them that it is possible to develop an effective strategy for reducing and hopefully eliminating the growing conflict between business and government that is of little benefit to anyone — business, government, or society.

The Decline in Business-Government Confidence

According to CEOs, the reasons for the deterioration of business relations with Ottawa during the 1970s fall into two broad categories: first, the failure of business to have sufficient impact in the determination of the public interest; and, second, the failure of the govenment to operate effectively. The reason for the failure of the private sector to have a significant impact is associated with (1) an inability to communicate effectively, (2) an ineffective consultative process, (3) a lack of understanding on the part of business of the political process, and (4) a lack of ability to communicate the position of business on various issues to the public. Government's failure is attributed to a breakdown in the government decision-making process, which is reflected most strongly in its incapacity to manage the economy.

Given the fact that the Liberal governments of the 1970s established the most comprehensive, certainly the most complex, system of consultation ever attempted with the various sectors in the economy, it is somewhat surprising that CEOs believe one of the reasons for the decline in business-government relations is the lack of consultation.[2] For consultation to be credible, however, "the results of the action must be apparent in the action of the government" and CEOs believe that even though they may be talked to, they are not listened to, for "although the PM had a few meetings with a select group of businessmen which is helpful, ... I doubt that this resulted in a change in any of the PM's philosophies or modified legislation," or as another stated, "the Ottawa bureaucrats are just going through the motions of providing an audience, having no intention of departing from their predetermined positions. It seems they don't want to listen. . . ." Or as yet another executive put it, "government will only listen to business when they believe it will affect their political survival. . . ."

Some CEOs were concerned about who business communicated with and how they did it. As one expressed it, "the ultimate report to the minister is coloured by staff viewpoints, and often influenced by the opinions of consultants who do not have business expertise." Because of this, "business-government interaction should go on at all levels of the corporation and not exclusively at the CEO level . . ." and not enough of this has taken place. Moreover, the very problem of how to communicate has become more difficult, for "as government has broadened its responsibilities and more and more government departments have become involved in economic areas, contact between the business and political world has become much more complex. . . ." In addition, as another CEO pointed out, "[business leaders] are self-conscious about engaging in debate with politicians because their language is different . . . and politicians probably see businessmen as tough, selfish, and inarticulate. . . ."

Underlying almost all CEOs' views about communication is the "negative attitude of business leaders to government. They are suspicious about governments, government activities, politicians, and civil servants. . . ." Or as another senior officer put it, "public officials and businessmen do not take each other seriously. Most businessmen have a low opinion of politicians, and even less of an opinion of civil servants, and similarly civil servants are not comfortable with businessmen. . . ." The fact is that all too often "distrust and lack of credibility are characteristic of the relationship between politicians and business. . . ."

Many executives believe that when they are arguing a case, they are viewed as putting forth the position of a vested interest and, therefore, their concepts are dismissed. Fully 75 per cent of CEOs believe that the "fact that business is assumed to speak as a vested interest group on *all* policy matters is fundamental to the problems between government and business."

But why should this be so? Surely business is no more of a special interest group than labour, or consumers, or native peoples, or any other group that attempts to influence policy. Indeed, it is less so than many of the special interest groups, such as pro-life, that are active in the corridors of the Parliament buildings. The explanation probably lies in the fact that business is perceived to be very powerful, but many executives think, rather, that the perception of business as a strong vested interest is something that is very much in the eye of the beholder. "Vested interests do exist in many areas, but I believe the case is often over-emphasized in the minds of government people" is not an unusual response from chief executives. Most businessmen believe that "the burden of proof that business can and usually does operate in the public interest seems to rest clearly with the private sector," primarily because the government and the public simply do not understand how business works.

On the other hand, according to some CEOs, businessmen simply react to issues, rather than propose solutions, and often spokesmen are out of touch with society's changes and expectations. Moreover, the views of many businessmen are often hackneyed (although often still valuable), for, as one noted, "business is really quite well organized to communicate its views to government and the public. The problem is what it communicates. . . . I just had a conversation with an Ottawa lawyer who said (in reference to the appearance of the Canadian Manufacturers' Association before the Cabinet), 'Oh well, of course, they will want to lower taxes, fire a bunch of civil servants, express themselves in favour of private enterprise, and ask the government to give Chrysler a big loan'. There is a certain stereotype to all business representation which makes it roll off the political back like water off the back of a duck. If, instead, the C.M.A. were to come forward some year with a brief in which they explained that they had worked out a set of rules that all foreign-owned companies had agreed to abide by in the national interest, or if they some year sponsored a study of corporate structure in Canada . . . and made recommendations as to how this structure could be improved both by legislation and through creative application of taxation, then I think politicians would sit up and take notice."

This position was reinforced by another CEO who noted that "too often ... the quality of advice offered from the businessmen exposes their lack of experience and sensitivity to the political process. As a result, their solutions are politically impractical. ..." Or as stated by another, "the political arm has a short-term approach and fails to understand how important business is to the economy ... but ... business is too narrowly focused and seldom has any comprehension of social, economic, and political issues that face the government. ..." Or, yet another, "business has difficulty in influencing policy because it does not understand the value systems of the bureaucracy and the political process, ... it does not accept the validity of ideas that come from outside its own intellectual circles. ..." And one suggests that "businessmen who are listened to in Ottawa, and have influence, are those who understand the system. ... With this in mind, perhaps leading candidates for senior positions in business and industry should be encouraged to do a stint in the civil service or politics. ..."

Finally, and very significantly, many CEOs suggested that because senior businessmen do not make their positions clear to the public, they lack support when they work with Ottawa. "Senior businessmen should voice political opinions. This is difficult in Canada, because top management is viewed as a political neuter with the result that the media and politicians will not allow them to express political opinions separate from the corporation ...," but it must be done. Or "businessmen must take active and constructive steps to explain to the public and, when necessary, defend their reasons and rights to become actively involved in public affairs ..." because "businessmen who are best understood by government are those who have gone out of their way to explain their position and have taken a strong public stand. ..." It is imperative that "management speak out on public matters, subject to corporate responsibility, presupposing adequate knowledge and support to keep the spokesman informed and up to date."

There are some who take an opposing view. As one CEO pointed out, "the public rarely reads the speeches of CEO's ... and, therefore, businessmen should work quietly behind the scenes ..., but they should themselves keep a low profile because, except for a few notable cases, they are generally misunderstood when speaking beyond their own peer group. ..."

It appears, therefore, that from the point of view of CEOs and directors of Canadian firms, the conflict between business and government has increased for five basic reasons.

First, businessmen have difficulty in making their case to the bureaucracy. Executives are coming to the conclusion that many in the bureaucracy simply do not understand how the business enterprise system operates.[3] At one time this was perceived by CEOs to be a problem of communication, but it is more and more thought to be the result of a fundamental lack of understanding and sympathy for the enterprise system by senior government officials.

Second is the problem of credibility. Many executives believe that when they are arguing a case, they are viewed as putting forth the position of vested interests and, therefore, their concepts are dismissed.

Third, many chief executive officers believe that they do not have sufficient understanding of the political process and the political pressures under which politicians operate to make a case that is effective. As one put it, "business is not politically involved, and government doesn't listen to those who aren't," or there is a lack of "understanding of each other's problems and an entirely different motivation in the decision-making process." In the final analysis, it is all a matter of "confidence, credibility, and understanding."

Fourth, many CEOs believe that business does not have a sufficient understanding of how decisions are made in the public sector and where power actually exists. Until this deficiency is overcome, they are certain that business will not have the impact it has every right to expect to have, and that the public believes it has, in the determination of policies.

Finally, many CEOs believe that a key reason for this decline in business-government confidence is the ineffectiveness of government in the area of decision making. As one states, "the real issues are the decision-making process in government, and the fact that the government is using eighteenth century management techniques in a twentieth century world . . .," or as another reported, "those responsible for developing policies base their decisions on theory and philosophy, rather than on business experience . . .," or "business-sector managers experience difficulty in dealing with ministers as a result of their inability to manage responsibly, and their lack of discretionary time to evaluate policy . . . indeed, businessmen are convinced that the government simply does not know, in many instances, what solutions it is seeking to apply to many particular problems. . . ." In government "there is no concern with cost effectiveness, and there is no sense of urgency in its decision-making process as it affects some major national issues that are of tremendous importance, that is, energy, transportation, trade, etc. . . ."

According to one CEO, "the ability of the corporation to serve the nation cannot be divorced from relevant policies applied by government. Corporations have no power other than their capacity to accomplish purposes that are in the national interest . . ., however, governments' policies, whether by design or chance, are capable of inhibiting and ultimately destroying corporations . . . through inadequate and sometimes inadvertent decision-making processes."

Business-Government Relations:
Who Is Responsible?

The responsibility for dealing with government is a function of the CEO of the corporation. He develops and carries out the strategy and it is one of his most significant tasks. The amount of time that Canadian CEOs devote to governmental activities, when such activities are defined in the broadest terms, that is, on issues that are not of direct concern to their firm or industry, varies greatly, ranging from zero to more than 50 per cent. The mean average is 15 per cent; the mode, 10 per cent. The amount depends upon whether there is a heavy amount of legislation before Parliament and to some extent on what issues are of national importance. All executives found it difficult to estimate the time with accuracy, but most thought that it was increasing. The view of one, "I believe that a chief executive officer of a major corporation must be prepared to devote a good percentage . . . up to one third of his time to the interface with government depending on the issues at hand and the nature of his industry . . ." would sum up the general view, with the exception that few were prepared, or felt they needed to or should, spend as high a proportion of their time on public issues as did this executive.

Given the major impact that government is having on their operations, it is surprising that fewer than 10 per cent of the corporations have a senior officer with full-time responsibilities for business-government relations. Approximately 25 per cent of the firms assign the bulk of the work in the area, particularly staff work in terms of preparation of speeches, submissions to committees, briefs to Royal Commissions, and so on, to their public relations departments. In the rest of the firms, it is considered part of the responsibilities of the corporate affairs group, a group that also includes, in many cases, public relations. In general, government-corporate affairs are handled on an almost *ad hoc* basis with most activity being in response to some public initiative.

Few companies maintain full-time employees in Ottawa. Those that are heavily regulated do so because of the constant need to interrelate with the regulatory agencies. Some believe it is important to have someone in the Capital as a listening post, but by and large corporations prefer to deal through trade associations, or professional public affairs firms. Occasionally, according to some CEOs, once a person is in Ottawa for any length of time, he loses contact with the company, and others suggested that too often such employees become too much a part of the Ottawa bureaucracy.

Chief executive officers look upon dealing with government and influencing legislation as *their* function. And while they spend a good deal of their time in such activity, they are prepared, if they can be effective, to spend more. When asked how could government use their time and experience more effectively, 70 per cent simply replied, "by asking me." There is concern that after advice is given, it is not taken, but this is not nearly as troublesome to them as not being asked at all for opinions and advice on issues where they feel they have considerable expertise. Strangely enough, for a group who by and large are decision makers, there is a modest penchant for committee work. Several CEOs believe that involvement in special committees is a significant way to make important input. As some reported, "Let's have less data collection, and paper work; more advisory groups," and "I personally have served on a number of government committees and feel that this is a good opportunity for government to use the time and experience of businessmen. . . ." Unfortunately, many governments infrequently act on the findings of committees, and "more attention should be given to the consultative process . . ." are typical comments. In short, CEOs believe that there is a pressing need for more consultation and more listening by government to corporate views.

This wish for more consultation, however, seems more of a response to the desire to do something to improve the situation, rather than of true hope that consultation will actually lead to better results. When pressed, most felt that consultation alone would not do much to improve business-government relations. Indeed, there were some who felt that there may actually be too much apparent consultation. When all is said and done, slightly over 50 per cent of the CEOs believe that direct, personal dialogue with a minister or senior public servant is the most effective way to make progress. One-on-one on an issue is the preferred approach. As one CEO explained, "public policy can best be influenced by a senior officer of a corporation involved in ongoing interaction and dialogue with government" and "we believe that it is important to develop these relationships at times when there is no crisis between the corporation concerned and the government," or as another put it, best results are obtained "by achieving a personal relationship with both elected officials and senior members of the civil service, developing mutual confidence and opportunity to discuss national interest in the area of public policy."

Twenty per cent of the CEOs believe that they can be most effective with government by working closely with organizations such as the Business Council on National Issues (BCNI) and the C.D. Howe Institute. Still others mentioned trade associations, and a very few thought that there was nothing that worked. Another 20 per cent believe that they could be most influential by speaking out on issues, preferably in an objective and non-partisan manner, and the balance, less than 10 per cent, thought they personally could be most effective through direct political action.

The fact that only 10 per cent of CEOs believe that the appropriate strategy for business to influence public policy is through direct action is consistent with other findings about strategies for dealing with business-government relations, but it is not in harmony with what many businessmen, at least in the abstract, think needs to be done. According to a survey of 800 Canadian-based firms taken in 1978 by the Institute for Political Involvement, "over 46 per cent of the respondent firms support the principle of a political response to the growing intervention of the federal government in the economic system."[4] Moreover, according to the study, businessmen believe that "the political system provides the arena within which most vital issues will be resolved. . . . the social focus of our times [is that] the political institutions have gained dominance. . . . Government . . . sits as an invisible partner of every company. . . . Indeed, government policy can determine the survival of a company or an industry. . . . The challenge . . . of the modern business firm is how to contend in a society that turns increasingly to the political system for the resolution of both social and economic problems. . . ."[5] Further, they believe that they have the right, both as businessmen and as citizens, to be more deeply involved in the political process and they are certain that both society and business would benefit from greater interaction — society by receiving better government and business by becoming more sensitive to political and social change.[6]

In spite of this, only a small proportion of the firms in the survey (one in twelve) characterize their involvement in the political process as high,[7] and while many reasons are provided for such a small amount of activity in politics, the overwhelming "distinguishing characteristic of a politically sensitive company is the attitude of the Chief Executive Officer. Where company leaders, whether because of personal interest or insight into the changing role of business in society, place a high value on political participation, this attitude is manifested in policies and practices that encourage higher levels of involvement in the political system."[8] In short, there is considerable evidence to suggest that senior officers believe that political action is necessary, but very few are willing to become involved in it to a great degree.

Inasmuch as the traditional approaches, dealing with ministers and senior officials and working through trade associations, do not appear alone to be able to reverse the decline in business-government relations, perhaps a more direct political and public approach is necessary. This would, however, require a major change in attitude and approach on the part of the CEO, who sets the policy of the firm. What were the attitudes of CEOs about such an approach for himself and his corporation at the beginning of the 1980s?

The CEO
and Political Involvement

Does a person who becomes the chief executive officer of a major corporation have a responsibility to participate in politics beyond the usual requirements of good citizenship? Yes, according to 75 per cent of directors and senior executives of Canadian corporations participating in this study, but nearly all respondents qualify their answer. Very few believe that being a senior officer automatically qualifies one for entering politics, but if a CEO elects to do so he should certainly have the support of his board. Moreover, he should, according to most of his peers, carefully assess whether or not he has the characteristics necessary for a successful career in politics. Many believe that, by and large, CEOs are not cut out for the political life. In addition, because of increasing conflict-of-interest laws, and the public perception of the influence of business in politics, some believe that it is more difficult than it used to be to get actively involved.

Some executives of very large corporations think that not only is more direct political participation desirable, but inevitable. "For many of us this is becoming increasingly inescapable . . .," and it is a good thing, for "presumably a senior executive has attained his position because (among other things) he is aware of social, political, and economic issues affecting the country. This implies a level of consciousness that suggests that the usual requirements of good citizenship applying to an executive are more intense and broad than those of, say, a retired tradesman, in a small village." The fact is that most corporation executives believe that people with their background and training have an expertise and training that would be valuable in the governing process.

Those executives who think that senior businessmen should not get involved in politics base their conclusion on the fact that (1) senior officers cannot speak for their employees, stockholders, and/or board members, and yet because of their identification with the firm they lead, a connection will be made in the minds of the public between the position taken by the individual and the corporation — a connection that could be harmful to the firm; (2) senior officers, if they are doing an effective job for their firm, do not have the time to be in politics, and (3) the Canadian system of government is simply not structured to enable a person to move from a career as a CEO to government and then back again. The company cannot hold the position open while the CEO is temporarily gone, and there is little inclination for companies to consider experience in government as a major plus factor when looking for CEOs. Consequently, the two careers do not mix.

In short, the current generation of senior executive officers in major Canadian corporations are predisposed towards involvement in the political process, and presumably would not stand in the way of, indeed would encourage, active participation in the process by their colleagues, but there is little evidence to suggest that many are thinking of trading their private corporate responsibilities for political ones.

Given the fact that CEOs approve of political activity — and this can be defined by everything from voting to standing for election to contributing money — how do they sense their obligations with respect to specific political issues? For example, what is their attitude about publicly endorsing candidates for political office? Interestingly, on this issue there is an equal split: half think they should, half think they should not.

Those who believe that it is appropriate to endorse worthwhile candidates state that it is simply an exercise in good citizenship, and see no reason why they should not work actively and publicly for the person whom they think will serve the nation best. Such endorsements should be made, however, not by the corporation, but by the CEO in his capacity as a citizen.

On the other hand, those who think it is inappropriate for the CEO to endorse a candidate believe that it is risky from the point of view of the company they head to do so, because it may (1) alienate customers, (2) alienate politicians, (3) alienate some voters and therefore have a negative impact, and finally (4) come back to haunt a company in terms of regulation enforcement.

While CEOs are split as to whether or not they should endorse particular candidates at election time, there is high support for the proposition that they should take an active role in political parties. Over 80 per cent of all respondents believe that they should do so because it is a function of good citizenship, and most believe that in terms of policy formulation and organizational needs, they have much to offer the parties. There is concern, however, that pre-emption by one party can create difficulties, and several suggest that instead of being involved in the political process through working with one party, they should try to influence all parties — which probably means they would influence none.

One of the significant advantages of being involved in a political party, particularly if the involvement is at a local level, is that it enables a person to have some influence on the selection of candidates for political office. What do CEOs think of the quality of federal politicians? Practically all know some very good members as well as poor ones, but approximately half believe that federal politicians are on balance only ordinarily capable in performing their jobs, 25 per cent think that they are poor, and 25 per cent, that they are good. The basic problem of Members of Parliament, according to the respondents, is not their sincerity or energy, but their woeful lack of training and knowledge in so many areas where they have to make decisions.

Moreover, in many respects they are prisoners of the system and, therefore, totally ineffective in bringing change. In general, one stated, "they are a cross-section of society reflecting the common denominator of the electorate. A few are outstanding, many average, and some mediocre to poor," but perhaps the truest sentiment was captured in a response of a former businessman, "hardworking, dedicated, and ineffectual. . . ." There was also concern expressed that, overall, the House is not representative: there are not enough businessmen and too many lawyers serving in Parliament.

Given the fact that CEOs are concerned about the performance of government, it is not astonishing that they believe more businessmen should run for political office. In fact, over 85 per cent of all respondents favoured the suggestion. However, as one put it, "in an ideal world, yes — in the real world, not likely to happen," and given all the qualifications put forth by businessmen on the answer, this seems a fair assessment. While CEOs favour more businessmen running, they almost unanimously point out some reason why it is difficult for businessmen to do so. Near the top of the list is the financial sacrifice, followed closely by concern about having to give up all business connections and hope of further progress in business after being in politics. In addition, some point out that it is "not worth the hassle."

Several CEOs suggested that businessmen do not have the skills essential for successful political careers, "no [they should not run because] I believe the qualities that make for success in business and politics are mutually exclusive," and while most CEOs want more businessmen to run, in their hearts they seem to harbour this same view. When asked, "Do you think businessmen, in general, are effective as politicians?" 75 per cent said no. Nearly all believe that businessmen have neither the patience nor talent for dealing with the public that are essential for political success, although they believe that businessmen do have the capacity to learn such skills.

Assuming that running for office is out of the question, can and should CEOs make a contribution to politics in some other manner? The answer is clearly "yes." Ninety per cent of CEOs believe that businessmen should publicly try to influence political decisions. As one points out, "we must, to stay in business." Again, however, most believe that they should do so as individuals exercising their rights and duties as citizens and not in their capacity as leader of their organization. On balance, 80 per cent believe that it is appropriate that they endorse legislation that is not directly concerned with their firm or industry, although most qualify their answer. The majority stress that any endorsement should be "with care, that is, clearly a personal, in contrast to a corporate, opinion," and only on issues about which the executive is particularly knowledgeable.

Another way of attempting to influence legislation is by testifying before a committee of the House of Commons. Many CEOs do this when legislation affecting their industry is being considered, but should they appear on legislation that is not directly concerned with their firm or industry? Seventy per cent say yes. The general view is that if the legislation is of importance to the country, and if they are invited to appear, they should do so. Again, they believe that it is important that they testify as individuals, not as CEOs.

Clearly CEOs in Canadian firms realize that politics is an inescapable element in their business, and they accept the fact that they must be involved one way or another in the political process. They are prepared as individuals to attempt to influence legislation that goes beyond their own business or industry. They will endorse legislation, testify about it, and try to get it passed or blocked. Moreover, while they are not overwhelmed by the quality of federal politicians, they give them high marks for effort and integrity, although they would like to see more businessmen in Parliament in spite of the fact that they do not believe businessmen are good politicians. Finally, they are enormously conscious of the difference between their responsibilities as individuals and as CEOs, and they are nervous about the two positions being confused.

How do these findings correlate with the conclusion that only 10 per cent of CEOs believe that working through the political process is the most effective manner of influencing public policy? The answer is in the word "effective." Clearly CEOs all realize that they manage in a political environment and, therefore, they must respond to that environment in the traditional manner. Moreover, traditionally, Canadian businessmen have appeared before parliamentary committees and have had some modest participation in political parties. But, by and large, the majority of Canadian CEOs believe that they can be more effective in changing the direction of public policy through influencing elected officials and public servants than by taking a high public profile on issues. And, of course, they feel they should exercise their responsibilities as citizens in contributing to the normal operations of the political process. As individuals they feel they should participate in the process, but what do they think that the corporations that they head — as corporations — should do in the political sphere?

The Corporation in Politics

If there is one underlying theme in the position of CEOs with respect to political involvement, it is that such involvement must be undertaken by the CEO as an individual, and not in his capacity as head of a firm. Does this mean that corporations, as corporations, have no political role? Well, not exactly. In fact, 50 per cent of the CEOs responded that corporations should be politically active on issues that are not of direct concern to them, but there was considerable hedging on the matter. Most felt that if a corporation was to speak out as a corporation on an issue, that the issue had to be one of broad public importance, such as national defence or taxation. Some CEOs suggested that "speaking out" should be part of the entire package of activities undertaken by a corporation as a function of its social responsibilities, and not as a separate political act.

Those opposed to the idea of corporations taking a stand on political issues, as corporations, do so because they believe a corporation is made up of many constituencies — employees, customers, shareholders, management, directors — and it is presumptuous to believe that there is one position on any truly significant issue that adequately reflects all constituents' views. Finally, there was considerable concern about the usefulness of corporations being actively involved in politics. Many CEOs feel that the impact could be negative.

If a corporation, as a corporation, is to be politically involved, what should it do? Should corporations, for example, endorse positions before and/or during elections? Slightly more than half of the CEOs and directors think that they should not, and almost all believe that if it is to be done, it should be done before, not during, an election. The major reasons for not endorsing legislation are (1) "public endorsations can in some circumstances damage the future of the company," (2) it is difficult to really know the entire corporation's view: employees, stockholders, et al., and (3) it does not do much good. "Endorsement" is in the view of one CEO "probably too late" or "they should establish their positions independent of election pressures"; or "as individual companies, no, but if a consensus can be developed in a trade association, yes"; and "generally speaking I don't think corporations should get involved in politics outside of informing politicians and the public on matters that affect their particular firm or industry."

On the other hand, there is almost unanimity among CEOs of large corporations that if someone from the organization wants to stand for elected office, he should be granted leave to do so, and if elected, he should be granted leave to serve. This is in marked contrast to the findings of the Institute for Political Involvement that indicated that only 39 per cent of the firms surveyed had specific policies with respect to leave for running for political office or participating in a campaign, and only 27 per cent had any type of programme designed to facilitate employees' involvement in the political process. In fact, 12 per cent had policies designed to prevent such involvement, and 9 per cent of the firms would refuse an employee permission to run for public office. If an employee did run, and win, 59 per cent of the firms would give the winner a leave of absence, although only 14 per cent would do so automatically, and 19 per cent would require the employee to resign. The balance had no policy on this issue.[9]

In contrast to these opinions, CEOs would actively encourage anyone who seemed to have the capacity, and the interest, to get directly involved in politics. Comments ranged from "yes, it is a duty" to "I think that any assistance that can be given to any candidate should be provided by the company he works for." However, most report that there should be some time limit on the length of leave of absence — two elections seemed to be the maximum — and there is concern about fitting a person who has been away from the organization for a number of years back into the mainstream of the company.

There is not unanimity, but strong support for the proposition that companies should have a well-developed political education programme. For example, 75 per cent of the CEOs believe that it is proper to arrange for politicians to speak to employees on company time. As to be expected, they believe that this must be done on a non-partisan basis, "with balance and discretion," for "I think it is helpful to the democratic process if corporations facilitate their employees hearing all candidates. Otherwise, there is a danger of them being unilaterally propagandized by one party that gains access to them through the union" and "[this] is a positive part of an active political involvement policy for corporations. I endorse it enthusiastically." Naturally, sensitivity must be applied to "equal time" during election campaigns, and in non-election times, "the issues and the politicians involved must be weighed very carefully" are typical views.

Those opposed to arranging for political meetings simply do so on the grounds that it is not necessary: "I think politicians can speak without any assistance," and "my experience with this is that it never works out."

In addition to making it easier for employees and officers of the corporation to seek political office and to increase the political awareness of employees by having political meetings on the corporation's premises, it is possible for the corporation to try to reach a larger audience through direct appeal — through advocacy advertising. What do Canadian CEOs think about influencing public opinion through advertising about issues that are not of direct concern to the firm or industry? Almost 60 per cent think that it is a poor idea. Basically they believe that it is not useful to do so because it does not do much good, that it is a questionable use of resources, that there are other better ways of getting the same message across, and as one executive put it, "I doubt that this would be . . . acceptable to the shareholders."

On the other hand, those who support the concept do so with some vigour: "why not . . . labour does it . . . many industries are asleep regarding public relations," "yes . . . it gives the public additional information to act on. . . ."

Whether or not one believes in advocacy advertising is associated with whether or not one believes that corporations, as corporations, should invest in achieving higher political profiles, and only 42 per cent of Canadian CEOs in large publicly held companies think that they should. However, even those who think that they should, want to do so with caution. For example, there is concern about appearing too partisan. As one CEO put it, "in today's society most issues are political in the broadest sense. Corporations cannot merely discuss economic issues. I think that corporate involvement in the political process in this broad way should be encouraged, but I am not in favour of major corporations achieving high profiles because of partisan political involvement," or "yes, but care should be taken to avoid a wholly partisan position." Those who are opposed to investing funds to increase the political profile of a company feel that "the profile is too high already," or "most companies have a higher political profile than they would desire," or "at present the environment in Canada would mitigate against this because in my view the credibility of corporations is not what it should be."

In summary, it is clear that CEOs of large corporations in Canada are conscious of the responsibility that corporations, as corporations, have to their employees, as these responsibilities relate to politics. They will grant leave for people to seek elected office, they will grant extended leave for people who are elected to serve, they encourage discussion of political events by members of the organization through meetings with politicians, and so forth. Where there is real concern is the extent to which the corporation, as a corporation, should go public on political issues. They are nervous, as well as sceptical, about the efficacy of advocacy advertising, or of the corporation developing a strategy to influence public opinion through endorsing specific legislation or taking strong public stands on general, as opposed to specific, political issues that do not directly affect the corporation. Part of this reluctance stems from their perception of the corporation as more than simply a body that is owned by the shareholders. Rather it is perceived as a body of many parts — employees, management, shareholders, directors — and they do not really know how such a polyglot group can speak with one voice about broad political issues.

While this broadened perception of what the corporation actually consists of has significant implications for management's attitudes and approaches to the usual questions of corporate social responsibility, interestingly enough it limits the possibility of the corporation in the area of political activity. Is it not a paradox that the acceptance in the broadest sense of social responsibility, in response to perceived political pressures, may in fact, by making it less possible for corporations to take strong political stands, lead to a smaller role for the corporation in the modern economy?

It is clear that the majority of CEOs are conscious of their own responsibilities and those of the corporations that they manage in the fulfilment of responsibilities in the democratic process. What they have not faced up to is the question of the responsibility of the corporation and the CEO in helping to determine the public interest in a changing and complex society. They believe, even with the substantially larger role of government in the economy, that the most effective method for having an input into the determination of the public interest is through dealing with ministers and officials on a one-on-one basis and working through their traditional channels. While they recognize the growing political influence in the decisions that they must make, there is little belief that a high-profile, direct political action strategy is essential for CEOs or corporations. But is this true? Are the strategies of the past going to be effective in the future? Are the methods and the mechanisms of the past adequate in a society with growing public action? Can CEOs make an effective input into the determination of the public interest in the future in the same manner as they have done in the past?

Notes

[1] Statistics in this chapter, and all quotations unless otherwise noted, are from a survey of CEOs and directors. See Appendix A.

[2] In an effort to overcome some of the perceived difficulties in communication with the private sector, the government, through the Department of Industry, Trade and Commerce, organized a formal consultative process in the spring of 1978 that involved some 23 task forces from 21 manufacturing sectors plus the construction and tourist industries, involving more than 600 people from 305 corporations. While not a great deal appeared to come out of the process, it certainly was a major effort. For a complete discussion of the procedure and its results, see Marc C. Baetz, "The Purpose and Influence of a Canadian Exercise in Formal Consultative Industrial Planning," Ph.D. dissertation, University of Western Ontario, 1980.

[3] Isaiah A. Litvak, "The Ottawa Syndrome: Improving Business/Government Relations," *Business Quarterly* 44 (Summer 1979), p. 25.

[4] Institute for Political Involvement, *A Report on the Prospects for Increased Involvement of Business People in the Canadian Political System* (Toronto: Institute for Political Involvement, 1978), p. 13.

[5] *Ibid.*, pp. 1–2.

[6] *Ibid.*, p. 13.

[7] *Ibid.*, p. 10.

[8] *Ibid.*, p. i.

[9] *Ibid.*, pp. 6–7.

Dealing with Government: Strategies

4

Contemporary Canadian CEOs know that the ability of the organizations that they manage to achieve their goals, indeed perhaps even to survive, depends more and more on external forces, particularly political ones, over which they, as managers, have little, if any, control. Consequently, they have to spend more of their time on the development of a social and political strategy for their corporation, the underlying purpose of which is to match the activities of the firm to the environment in such a way that they are in reasonable harmony.

During the past ten years, all evidence indicates that this matching has not been achieved and, indeed, that instead of improving, relations between the private and public sectors are getting worse. Consequently, existing management strategies for dealing with governments clearly are in need of review, and perhaps entirely new ones will be necessary in the years ahead. At the very least, serious assessment of the relationship is essential.

Since the end of World War II, the basic strategies of business for dealing with government may be classified into two major and one minor categories. The first are what is known as (1) the mutual co-operation with division of responsibility clearly defined; and (2) the issue-by-issue. The second, which has only become recognized in the past decade and which is still not widely accepted, might be defined as (3) the political approach. What are the characteristics and the strengths and weaknesses of each of these possible strategies for the turbulent times ahead?

Why Not Mutual Accommodation?

Proponents of this approach believe that it is possible — and valuable — to define the role of government and other sectors of society in the economy through some type of mutual planning. Underlying such reasoning is the conviction that together business and government can work out a social contract that when put into effect will lead to greater productivity, more growth, less industrial unrest, and less regional disparities in income. It is based on the fundamental notion that the government should establish the goals and formulate the strategies

for the economy, and the private sector should implement them.[1]
Working towards this type of relationship, it is contended, should be
the task of all strategies of business for dealing with government and
of government for dealing with business.

Moreover, it is argued that such an approach is particularly
appropriate in Canada "because private-sector corporations are less
dependent on the shifting winds of political parties, penalties, and
philosophies in a country like Canada than many are inclined to
believe."[2] This is true because in Canadian society corporations are
not only the primary generators of wealth, but they are perceived by
the public to be so, and the public wants wealth. Therefore, it is
contended that as long as corporations do what they are supposed to
do, namely provide goods and services, they can always arrange an
effective accommodation with any government.

Opponents of this view maintain that there are several fundamental
flaws in the position. First, the enormous increase in government
regulations and laws, in and by itself, is making it more difficult for
corporations to produce effectively. It is a common complaint of
executives that government actions have markedly decreased the
effectiveness of corporations as wealth producers. Second, there is
some question as to whether or not society's central goal is the
production of more wealth, at any cost. Third, the public does not
automatically believe that corporations are the only way, or indeed
the best way, to produce wealth. The example of the oil companies and
the public attitude about their activities is instructive on this point.
And fourth, there are people in positions of authority — decision
makers — who do not believe that the private sector is the most
effective way to produce wealth. To the extent that any of these factors
are in play, the capacity of the corporation to operate is limited and the
role of government is likely to increase.

Few would challenge the idea that co-operation and accommodation
are normally more effective and always more pleasant than confrontation. But a necessary condition for any effectiveness of such an
approach is shared belief in how the goals of society can be achieved;
and many CEOs are convinced that unlike the 1950s and 1960s, such
shared values no longer exist between public and private decision
makers. Indeed, it is suggested that there is no way that they now
could because (1) few if any of the key decision makers in Ottawa have
had any experience in the private sector, (2) few if any CEOs have had
experience in the federal government, and (3) the isolation of Ottawa
physically, economically, and culturally from the rest of the nation
feeds the capacity for separate viewpoints. The reality is that whereas
CEOs are convinced that the public interest is best served by an
effective private sector, many senior government officials believe that
government can solve problems more effectively than business.[3] A

close congruence of views simply no longer exists, and without such a congruence it is difficult to develop a programme of mutual accommodation and co-operation on truly significant issues.

The differences are also exacerbated by the fact that few businessmen have any close understanding of the problems that public servants — and to a lesser extent politicians — must contend with, and indeed, hold the well-publicized view that most bureaucrats are inefficient and ineffective.

Whether or not this antagonism — almost mistrust — between the public and the private sectors is real or imagined, peripheral or permanent, it matters not. The evidence indicates that the trust and similarity of values that characterized dealings between government and business in the 1950s and part of the 1960s is no longer present. For example, on such a fundamental question as the development of energy, there is profound and basic disagreement between the public and private sectors as to whether the production of oil should be the responsibility of private or Crown corporations. Without a common set of values, it is impossible to develop an effective social contract.

However, attitudes do change over time — indeed, one of the purposes of effective business-government management is to narrow the gap between differing views; but the problem that government may not be able to fulfil its part of the contract is more difficult to resolve. For a variety of reasons — the complex changes in our society, alterations in the decision-making processes of government, and the amount of responsibility that citizens have asked governments to undertake — governments in the 1970s have not been able to accomplish many of the things they set out to do. Consequently, the efficacy of a mutual planning strategy must be assessed not only in terms of what things each segment of society should do, but what indeed they can do. To expect government to take on the additional task of defining rather specifically future goals and strategies, when it is finding it difficult to fulfil the responsibilities it has already undertaken, is hoping for a great deal. At the very least, it indicates that the likelihood of success from some new type of mutual accommodation or co-operation approach is not likely to be very great.

In addition, the adoption of a "mutual co-operation strategy" at a period of time when the central issue, from the point of view of CEOs, is the extent of government involvement in the economy, flies directly in the face of one of the most widely accepted explanations of why governments grow: the incremental theory.[4] According to the incrementalists, the rapid increase in the size of government has resulted not from any plan or ideology, but rather as a consequence of hundreds of independent actions taken in response to perceived problems. When a problem is brought to Ottawa by a portion of the electorate, the immediate reaction of the government is to attempt to solve it — and this usually means more government activity, often legislation. Every action in turn brings its own increase in rules and regulations — and this increase in rules and regulations often results in a situation that calls for more legislation, and so on. If the proper interrelationship between business and government is perceived to be that of co-operative partners in some type of mutual planning, it is almost inevitable, although neither by design nor intention, that the role of the government in the economy will increase, not decline.

To outline the problems is not to suggest that co-operation is undesirable. To the contrary, our entire society works on the concept of mutual trust and interchange of views and values. However, given the experience of the 1970s, if the goals of private-sector management are to limit, because they believe it is in the public interest to do so, the expansion of government in the economy, the "mutual co-operation strategy" will not achieve that aim. Other methods of playing a role in determining the public interest need to be found.

The Issue-by-Issue Approach

The most frequent strategy used by business to influence government action in the post–World War II period has been the issue-by-issue approach. As the name implies, in its simplest version, it means that business reacts to individual initiatives of the government as those initiatives are introduced. The ones that are perceived to be detrimental to the corporation or an industry — and the public interest — are opposed. It implies no grand strategy: it is simply as it states, an approach that calls for dealing with issues as they develop.

The basic requirements for such a strategy are (1) an early-warning system that alerts managers about what the government intends to do, and (2) reasons that will convince the proponents of the proposal, if it is deemed detrimental, to withdraw or change it. The process requires close interrelationship by business with all parts of the bureaucracy and the executive and legislative branches of government. Such relationships are developed and maintained by trade associations, professional business-government consulting firms, and by chief executive officers and senior officers of corporations. Indeed, trade association officials stress that one of their major duties is to keep close to the members of the bureaucracy so that they may spot the early evolution of ideas and inform their members about any developments that may influence their activities.

The issue-by-issue approach is based on the proposition that the transmission of appropriate, useful information at the appropriate level of the bureaucracy will in fact stop an inappropriate concept from being enacted. And indeed, it probably will. Governments do not want to pass legislation that in its own terms is ineffective. They want to minimize the side-effects of any particular act on individuals and organizations that the legislation is not supposed to affect. They want to be certain that legislation does what it is designed to do, that regulations regulate the actions they are designed to regulate, that tax rulings are equitable, that tariff enforcement is sound, and so on. On such issues, there is no question that working with the bureaucracy on a case-by-case approach is not only effective, but essential.

But is it effective on major policy questions? Is it effective in terms of influencing the general economic structure of the nation? Has it served the business community and the people of Canada well by creating an environment for economic well-being? The answer to these questions is probably no.

An underlying assumption of the strategy is that policy flows in government from the bottom up. In many cases this is indeed true, but with respect to significant issues it often is not. Moreover, on very important matters the influence of even the most senior departmental public servants is limited. While it is true that ministers look to their deputies for advice[5] — and giving advice is a major function of senior public servants — if a minister and a government are determined to follow a particular line of action, no amount of intervention at any level of the bureaucracy at any time will stop such action, as, for example, the fate of the Canadian edition of *Time Magazine* illustrates. In spite of an intensive effort on the part of *Time* to maintain tax advantages for advertisers in its Canadian edition similar to those for advertisers in *Reader's Digest,* when the leadership of the Liberal Party decided the matter against *Time,* there was nothing that anyone in the bureaucracy could do about it.[6]

The *Time* case was not fundamental in terms of the future of the Canadian economy, but the evolution of policies for energy are. When Prime Minister Clark came to power, his government had the view that the goals of Canadian energy policy should, in the simplest of terms, be (1) to achieve energy self-sufficiency in all types of energy, including oil, by 1990; and (2) this should be done with as much reliance as possible on the private sector; moreover, (3) efforts should be made to lessen the conflict between the producing provinces and the federal government; and (4) policies should be followed to increase the proportion of the industry owned and controlled by Canadians. These goals differed from those of the former government to the extent that they marked a change from a policy of energy self-reliance, the cornerstone of the previous government's programme, to one of self-sufficiency, and they implied a different structure for the government-owned oil company — Petro-Canada.

The Clark government's policies were established at the top. The goals were not changed, and could not be changed, by members of the bureaucracy. Until all the people involved in the development of the Clark programme make public their positions on various aspects of the

Clark approach, one cannot say for certain what their positions may have been. There is, however, a belief by some that senior members of the Department of Energy, Mines and Resources were not in full sympathy with the Clark approach, particularly with respect to the privatization of Petro-Canada, and with respect to the role of the provinces in the development of Canada's energy resources. Be that as it may, it did not matter. The policy was established at the top, not in the department.

Under such circumstances, issue-by-issue working through the bureaucracy is irrelevant. While it is true that during the Clark administration senior officials in the Clark government met with industry representatives, such meetings were to determine how specific legislative actions would impact on activity in terms of the achievement of the already determined goals. The meetings had no impact on the goals themselves.

The essence of the issue-by-issue, fighting in the trenches approach is the hope of influence. It has in fact inherent within it no power other than the power of persuasion. Important as persuasion may be, it will always be limited, in highly controversial issues, to the amount of power (and to the politician this means real political power, votes) that those attempting to make the case can mobilize to support their position. This does not mean that the politician is an unprincipled, crass vote getter, uninterested in the fundamental welfare of the country. Rather it is a reflection of the fact that the politician sees his function of reconciling conflicting views about issues in such a way that the public interest, as perceived by the majority of Canadians, is satisfied. Sometimes the view is short term, because the politician's operational horizon is short term, and on some issues it is long, but it is always there, and properly so.

In addition, and most importantly, the most powerful arguments will not change the views of a government that fundamentally and basically disagrees with the approach that is being presented. There is no way in which the most skilful "case-by-case approach to the most influential decision maker about the efficiency of the private sector" will be relevant if the decision maker believes that there is no role for the private sector in the economy. There is absolutely no point in the CEO of an oil company trying to persuade a socialist that the oil industry can produce energy more efficiently and less expensively for the Canadian people than the government.

The fact is that the philosophy of the players in power makes a great deal of difference. If the decision makers perceive the private sector as ineffective or immoral, then the spokesmen for the private sector will get little support. If members of the bureaucracy believe that government can by and large solve problems better than institutions within the private sector, then the most persuasive argument will be of no avail.

Furthermore, it is quite incorrect for businessmen to believe that elected officials and bureaucrats assign a privileged position to business in society. They do not. Indeed, if anything, they perceive the power and role of business as substantially less significant than it was a few decades ago. For "since the 1950's there has been a massive shift in economic power from business to governments and the public interest groups they represent. The old economic power . . . is being replaced by a new economic power. . . . The old economic power was administered by private decisions from board rooms. The new economic power is administered by public decisions coming out of the political bargaining arena."[7] It would appear, therefore, that given the value systems in society and the changing relationship of business to government, reliance on the issue-by-issue approach may be inadequate, in terms of making an effective contribution in determination of the public interest.

This is not to suggest that there is no need for a continuing and close relationship between the bureaucracy and the business community. To the contrary, it is essential and of ever-increasing importance as the role of the government in the economy expands. However, it is not sufficient. In spite of ever increasing reliance on the issue-by-issue approach to business-government relations, the role of government in society has increased, the interface between business and government is marked by increasing tension, the economy is performing less efficiently, and the degree of direct government production of goods and services has expanded — and none of these things are the results that an effective strategy for dealing with government by corporations are expected to bring about. The one-on-one, face-to-face approach on particular issues no longer is effective — certainly not in dealing with major issues — and yet over half of all senior executives still believe that it is the best way of influencing public policy.

The Political Strategy:
Direct Action

A small number of CEOs, approximately 10 per cent, believe that if the private sector is to have an appropriate input into the determination of the public interest, it must do it through becoming more involved in the political process. Such an approach is highly contentious, however, and as a specific approach it is advanced with considerable trepidation. The essence of the argument for a political approach is simply that "if new economic power is administered by public decisions coming out of the political bargaining arena," then surely business must enter the political arena and exert political bargaining power to attempt to gain its points.[8]

Any strategy of some more direct type of political action by a corporation must be based on an understanding that in Canada (1) there is no fundamental ideological support for business, such as exists in the United States, (2) there is no special status for business with government, and (3) the changing decision-making process in government, the decline in power of individual ministers, the changing methods of financing elections, and a rapidly shifting power base make dealing in the political process a complex and a highly professional activity — an activity for which few businessmen are particularly well equipped either by experience or temperament. Consequently, when business attempts to utilize some type of political action strategy, it does not do so with any particular skill or success.

A strategy of political actions as a means of influencing the public interest may involve either a direct or indirect approach. The direct, of course, is simply that more businessmen become involved in the political process and seek election to positions of responsibility.

For a variety of reasons, this is the most significant and effective way to bring more of the private-sector viewpoint to the establishment of public policy. Regardless of what may be the perception, the policy line of a government is determined on major issues by elected people. There are a variety of ways of bringing influence to bear on the decision-making process — some direct, some indirect — but in the final analysis on significant issues someone has to act, and in Canada it is the members of the Cabinet and the legislature who make the final decisions. Nothing to which a Cabinet is adamantly opposed will be passed, regardless of the input of public servants, businessmen, or anyone else. Obviously, various groups have influence — there are trade-offs and adjustments — but in the last analysis it is the elected members, the Cabinet, and the Prime Minister who determine what actually happens.[9]

It is impossible to overstress the importance in the formulation of policy of the philosophy of the key people in the decision-making process. When decisions are made by people who have no fundamental understanding of how the market system operates, or who have no comprehension of the role of business in society, the results are different than when they are made by those who do. Moreover, when any one segment of society is not represented in the making of decisions, the public interest is not fully served. It can be, and is, correctly argued that a businessman in politics brings to his position all his prejudices and values that he acquired before entering politics and, of course, this is true, just as it is true of everyone — farmer, fisherman, school teacher, lawyer, or theologian — who enters politics. However, in the political decision-making process, views are challenged and debated and eventually, when consensus is reached, legitimized through the legislative process. If one sector's views are never put forward by someone in the decision-making process, the results for the community as a whole are less satisfactory than when all points of view are present at the time decisions are taken.

A second important reason for the use of a direct participation political strategy is that if businessmen believe that the public interest is best served by a strong and viable private business sector, part of the case for such a position must be made by businessmen who speak for the system as a whole. This is not to say that CEOs from their positions as CEOs of major corporations cannot contribute to the debates on public policy and that they will not have a significant impact on the public's perceptions and views, but their views will be less accepted than if they were made by a Member of Parliament. There must be people who understand the enterprise system speaking and working for the system, without at the same time having a vested interest in a single identifiable part of the system.

Indeed, one of the most serious problems that the private sector has is convincing the general public of the legitimacy of its views. And it is not astonishing that the public is sometimes confused because while business claims that it is concerned about the intervention of government in the economy, various business organizations and corporations are at the same time seeking some type of government assistance: lower taxes, higher tariffs, subsidies for research and development, grants for locating plants, and so on. To the public it is a paradox that business collectively argues that there is too much government and yet at the same time individually asks for more. How ironic it seems to the public that Lee Iacocca, while president of the Ford Motor Company, was a leading spokesman on the evils of government regulation, and two years later as president of Chrysler Corporation arranged the largest bail-out with government funds of a private corporation in history. The fact is, it is not a paradox. While at Ford, Iacocca's responsibility was to produce cars efficiently and effectively at the lowest possible price for the consumer, consistent with the laws of the land. Some of the laws and the regulations, he believed, were inappropriate and unnecessary in terms of doing what they were designed to do. Whether he was correct or not he clearly had the right to make his case, and as a senior officer of a major corporation affected by the laws, he had a duty to do so.

At Chrysler, his problem was quite different. The company, of which he was CEO, was going bankrupt and would, unless assisted, close. Again, it was clearly his duty as CEO to do everything possible, including going to the government for assistance, to work for the survival of the firm. It would be incredible if he did not. Indeed, it is inconceivable that the CEO of any organization would fail to take advantage of any opportunity presented by government to improve the performance of his firm. It would be inconsistent with reality if business executives did not seek assistance from their government in the performance of their duties. Such action by businessmen is exactly the same as the action of other members of society. Dairy farmers who sincerely believe that inflation and excessive government regulations are ruining the country work diligently to have the support price for milk raised. Labour leaders, worried about the relative decline in incomes of the members of their unions because of inflation, argue and strike for wage increases greater than the increase in productivity in the union. Academics concerned about excessive government spending apply, and usually receive, government grants to examine the impact of government spending on the economy. The list is endless, as any Member of Parliament knows.

The reality is that the broad public interest and the narrow private interest may or may not be the same. Moreover, what may be identified as identical private and public interests at one point in time may not be identical at another, and what may be perceived as being in the public interest for one section of an industry may be inimical to another section of the same industry. Raising the tariffs and placing quotas on the import of certain types of clothing protects parts of the Canadian textile industry (at least for a period of time) but at the same time is inimical to many small clothing retailers. Both groups are in business, both groups are in the private sector, both lobby the government diligently for action — one for protection through quotas, the other for abolition of quotas. Both are serving their own interests and both argue that what they are asking for is in the public interest and both in principle think the government does too much. Together they could be cited as yet another example that the private sector does not have a consistent position with respect to the role of government in society that is based on any fundamental philosophy about how the economy should function.

Such an argument can only be refuted effectively by people speaking for the system as a whole from a legitimate platform — and that is as an elected member of a legislature. If the position of the private sector in society is to be presented to the public, there must be spokesmen for the system, and this is best accomplished by business executives directly participating in the political process.

The third argument advanced for more direct political action by businessmen is that it makes communication between government and business easier, it leads to more understanding by businessmen of the political system, it should mean improved decision making in government, and it should lead to a greater understanding of business in society. These are the conclusions of political leaders, as well as businessmen. Both think that more businessmen in government would improve the quality of government.[10]

In spite of the case that can be made for direct political action — and more businessmen in public office — there are many reasons why it is not likely that such an approach is going to be taken by many CEOs. They will look, if they perceive the need for political action, for more indirect ways, both for their corporations and themselves, to participate.

The Political Strategy: Indirect Action

In general, corporate political action involves the mobilizing of support for positions that the business community applauds, or deplores, and corporations do not do this well. Although the success of the Canadian business community in changing some of the recommendations of the Carter *Report* on taxation, of delaying the introduction of a Competition Act, of causing the withdrawal of the Borrowers and Depositors Protection Act, for example, are cited as indications of their influence; the same legislation, or lack of it, is sometimes used to argue precisely the opposite.[11] Regardless, few would suggest that the increase in the intervention of the state in the economy is something that business has wanted, and yet it clearly has not had sufficient influence to stop it.

The major reasons for corporations' ineffectiveness in political action range from lack of perception to poor execution. Corporate managers, it is contended, often do not perceive the impact of a particular piece of legislation until it is too late to make any major changes in it; they do not put their views forward competently to the government; and they do not know how the system works. All these criticisms may be true,[12] but it is difficult to understand why this should be so with the possible exception of the charge that business does not understand how government works. There is in place in Ottawa a network of trade associations and consultants who constantly monitor the operation of government, the changing of power of decision makers, and the always shifting political climate. Indeed, the argument could be made that there are almost too many sources of information about government activities.

It is more likely that mistakes are made not in perception or execution, but in the interpretation of the results. In a relatively fast moving and changing environment, it is difficult to forecast the consequences of decisions. Moreover, errors are made, not because CEOs do not know what is planned but because businessmen are sometimes naïve in their dealings with politicians. Simply because a politician or a bureaucrat listens to an argument does not mean that he believes it. In fact it is part of a politician's task to listen to all positions on all questions and, while doing so, to keep everyone satisfied. Ministers, in particular, are very busy, their calendars are crowded, and the last thing they want to do, or indeed will do, is spend a good deal of time debating points with a visitor. The normal practice is to hear the argument, thank the presenter, and turn any item that needs immediate action over to an assistant. Consultation does not mean agreement, and even agreement does not guarantee action.

The only test that can be applied to the impact of a contact is what in fact happens. If the proposal presented is in harmony with the general view of the recipient, it is probable that it will have influence; if it is not, it is doubtful that any amount of persuasion will make any difference — although the reception will be polite, warm, and the exchange of ideas deemed mutually beneficial.

Corporations, even if they decide to adopt some type of indirect political strategy, are also often less than effective in mobilizing political power because the firms within the industry are fragmented in their views. Consequently, government is not sure what the industry wants even in cases where it perceives the public interest would be best served by agreeing with industry. On many matters politicians do not have the competence, and they know it, to make decisions, and when they get conflicting advice from industry, their task is simply made more difficult. Moreover, it is especially difficult for politicians to accept the credibility and legitimacy of positions when, in fact, corporations in the same industry put forth apparently fundamentally conflicting positions on similar matters.

If business is to be political, it does have a large constituency to cultivate and to use: employees, customers, shareholders. But they cannot be mobilized for political action on the basis of narrow corporate interests on anything but certain specific occasions that vitally impact on their interests. The in-pouring of form letters from employees or shareholders to a local Member of Parliament protesting a specific action is not likely to have much more than minimal effect on changing a policy. This is not to say that such action will not influence a politician, for nothing affects politicians more than the idea that they may win or lose votes on an issue, but a blatant special interest plea is unlikely to have more than a temporary impact.

If business is to use an indirect political approach in its attempt to have an effective input into the determination of the public interest, it has to develop creditable political positions. In the final analysis, it is impossible to win on issues in politics without mobilizing a constituency, but it cannot be mobilized without consistent positions that reflect the public interest and without the utilization of professional skills, many of which do not appear to be present in many Canadian corporations.

Choosing a Strategy:
The CEO's Dilemma

If the leaders of the private sector are to have an effective input into the determination of the public interest — and it is imperative that they do for effective operation of the political process — then corporations must adopt new approaches in dealing with government. For a variety of reasons the face-to-face, issue-by-issue approach does not appear to be as effective as it once was in influencing major policy positions of government; the mutual co-operation approach, while laudable, does not appear to be effective; and the direct political action approach, while useful, is to a very large degree impracticable except for a handful of executives.

And yet, important as it may be to the very survival of a firm, there is some indication that the development of effective business-government relations strategies is not always a top priority of management. Paradoxically, in some corporations, development is held back because business-government relations are the responsibility of the CEOs, and their close advisers, who know little about how to react to situations created by government. Should a key executive appear before a committee of the House of Commons? Should there be advertising about an issue? Should an alternative view be put forward? Should the issue be ignored? Will a small problem in a provincial legislature escalate into a national problem? Quite often the capacity for answering these and similar questions simply is not present.

In addition, focusing on selecting a strategy is delayed by the fact that many CEOs do not want to deal with external problems and consider them peripheral to their major function of operating the corporation. And this is not astonishing because for years executives have had "to fight constantly for market share, anticipate customers' needs, provide timely delivery, produce superior products, price them competitively, and assure the retention of customer loyalty . . .," as well as deal with automation and unions, retain their competitive position, satisfy stockholders "and generate sufficient retained earnings. . . ." No wonder they have been inclined "to treat early Post-industrial signs . . . [such as] . . . inflation, growing governmental constraints, dissatisfaction of consumers, invasion by foreign competitors, technological breakthroughs, changing work attitudes . . . as a distraction."[13]

The result of all this is that many corporations do not have strategies, implicit or otherwise, for dealing with the issues created by government and other changes in the environment. When something happens that impinges on the corporation, the reaction is to temporize, delay, and hope that the situation will go away; and if all else fails, to fire off some response without adequate analysis. And yet at some point, either explicitly or implicitly, the CEO must choose a strategy for his firm. He has the responsibility of maintaining some type of congruence between the goals of his firm and the goals of society, and he has a responsibility to input into the determination of the collective goals of society.

Notes

[1] William A. Dimma, "Government, Business, Labor: Some Future Directions," *Business Quarterly* 41 (Summer 1976), p. 48.

[2] W.A. Macdonald, "Corporate Needs and Public Expectations," Speech delivered to the Conference Board in Canada, Toronto, 6 March 1980, p. 5.

[3] Isaiah A. Litvak, "The Ottawa Syndrome: Improving Business/Government Relations," *Business Quarterly* 44 (Summer 1979), pp. 24–27.

[4] Charles E. Lindblom, "The Science of 'Muddling Through'," *Public Administration Review* 19 (Spring 1959), p. 86.

[5] Twelve of twenty former ministers reported using their deputies as their major source of advice.

[6] For an extensive study of the *Time* case, up to the first tax amendments for foreign periodicals published in Canada, see Isaiah A. Litvak and Christopher J. Maule, "Interest-Group Tactics and the Politics of Foreign Investment: The Time–Reader's Digest Case Study," *Canadian Journal of Political Science* 7 (December 1974): 616–29.

[7] Donald H. Thain, "The Mistakes of Business in Dealing with Politics and Government," *Business Quarterly* 44 (Autumn 1979), p. 48.

[8] William M. Lee, Speech delivered to the Toronto Ticker Club, 17 October 1975, p. 4.

[9] This is not to suggest that the process is clean and precise — indeed, it is not. See Chapter 6.

[10] Institute for Political Involvement, *A Report on the Prospects for Increased Involvement of Business People in the Canadian Political System* (Toronto: Institute for Political Involvement, 1978), pp. 12, 20.

[11] Andrew Roman, "Comments" on W.T. Stanbury, "Lobbying and Interest Group Representation in the Legislative Process," in *The Legislative Process in Canada: The Need for Reform,* edited by W.A.W. Neilson and J.C. MacPherson (Montreal: The Institute for Research on Public Policy, 1978), p. 215.

[12] Thain, *op. cit.*, pp. 48–50.

[13] H. Igor Ansoff, "The Changing Shape of the Strategic Problem," in *Strategic Management: A New View of Business Policy and Planning,* edited by Dan E. Schendel and Charles W. Hofer (Boston: Little, Brown, 1979), p. 33.

Dealing with Government: Tools and Tactics

5

In the 1950s, the strategic problem for many CEOs was simply to clearly identify the business they were in and to assess the strengths and weaknesses of their firms. Changes in the environment were quite predictable, and those that did occur normally impacted on activities with which management had always, at least derivatively, been concerned such as raising capital, expanding into new markets, developing new products, and acquiring firms; and the management tools they used for dealing with environmental changes were not particularly different from those they had always used — capital budgeting, measuring the rate of return on investment, and so on. When, as was the case in the early post–World War II period, there are reasonably predictable threats to the organization from environmental changes, it is possible to do some planning by traditional management methods to offset the consequences.[1] However, when, as happened in the 1960s and 1970s, the changes that take place are totally unexpected and the time to react to them is short, the traditional methods for dealing with change may be totally inappropriate, as the automobile industry in North America found, for example, after OPEC was formed.

No one can predict with certainty what is going to happen in the 1980s and 1990s, but it is a reasonable hypothesis that changes in the environment are going to occur — particularly political changes — that will require management responses that are new and different from those used in the past. Indeed, by the end of 1979, it was apparent that a major task of management in the 1980s was going to be to defend the legitimacy of the entire private sector as the principal producer of goods and services in society. In some industries — resources, communications, and finance — it may well be that management may have to develop strategies for survival of their firms, and this will require strategies and tactics for dealing with the social and political environments that are quite different from any used before.

Clearly, to assure the viability of their enterprises, CEOs must respond to social and political forces, and they must also accept the reality that they have a responsibility to help in the determination of the public interest. The CEO, in the latter part of the twentieth century, cannot claim that these are not part of his tasks as a manager. To the contrary, they could be among his most important functions.

The development of social and political strategies and tactics is a complex and difficult task. How should a corporation be organized to do so? What form should strategies take? What are the goals of strategies? Who should be responsible for their formulation? How should such work be staffed? How can opportunities created by changes in the political and social environments be identified and capitalized upon? How can, and should, the firm impact on the political environment? Choosing the appropriate strategies to use and what tactics to employ in dealing with government and other parts of the environment is truly one of the greatest challenges for management in the next decade.

Managing Social and Political Strategies

Determining a strategy for dealing with the political and social environments, and developing tactics for implementing it, is clearly a head office corporate function that must intimately involve the CEO of the firm.

While there are a number of ways in which the corporation may be organized to deal with the external environment, the most common is through a public affairs division or department headed by a senior vice-president who reports directly to the CEO, is a member of the principal management policy committees, and has broad terms of reference so that he has a major input into major corporate decisions that may, directly or indirectly, impact on the external environment. Obviously, the nature and size of the firm determines the appropriate size and organization of the public affairs division, but normally it has the responsibility for business-government relations, public relations, evolution of corporate social policy, and it has a significant role to play in the development of both the long- and short-term objectives of the firm.[2] Inasmuch as one of the principal objectives of management is to assure the profitability and survival of the firm in a sometimes unpredictable and threatening environment, the need for such an organized, co-ordinated, pro-active division within the company — as opposed to a reactive *ad hoc* capacity to respond to external changes and pressures — is self-evident.

In order for the public affairs function to be performed effectively, nine things are essential. First, the CEO must have some understanding of the public policy implications of what the firm does. Moreover, he must have a fundamental interest in dealing with such implications. While the majority of CEOs in large Canadian corporations accept this responsibility and perceive it to be one of their major tasks, it is not always true, for three major reasons, that they persistently and consciously follow through on their responsibilities. First, many do not like dealing with public affairs matters. They feel uncomfortable in the public environment, and in dealing with government officials. Second, they find it difficult to see the "bottom-line" implications of such work — it is the soft area of corporate management. Third, very few have much experience or training in the field.[3] In Canada, unlike in the United States, there is not substantial movement by senior management back and forth between the government and the private sector. Indeed, one of the most often-expressed concerns of private-sector people about entering into active politics or senior government service for a limited period of time is the fear that they will not be able to return to a senior-level position in the private sector. As the need for experience in dealing with the external environment becomes more and more critical, it is probable that this situation will change and that the private sector will actively seek people with public-sector experience for CEO and senior management positions. When that happens, the public affairs function in corporations will be given more attention.

Second, it is essential that senior management have good, accurate, and preferably early information about the forces external to it, which are, at present or in the future, going to affect materially the manner in which it operates. This involves systematic political analysis and, in the jargon of the day, "environmental scanning" so that emerging issues can be identified. While some major changes that may dramatically influence the future of the firm cannot be forecast, most major governmental policies are a considerable time in gestation. Indeed, the public policies of tomorrow can often be seen in the work of the scholars of today. Ideas do have consequences and the monitoring of their evolution and impact is critical to the health of the corporation. To be successful, a public affairs department has to monitor the environment, defined in the broadest sense.

Third, it goes without saying that the department must know the way in which the government makes its decisions, and who the significant policy makers are. This is not always obvious, particularly in the last decade, since a new system of decision making has been put into place in Ottawa and with it a new distribution of influence within the government and the bureaucracy. Without such knowledge, the expenditure of effort can be wasteful and indeed "counter-productive."

Fourth, the public affairs department, however organized, must be able to bring about responses within the company to the changes in the environment. It is meaningless to have information if that information is not used to modify the operations of the enterprise in response to changing conditions, and it should be recognized that to bring change is not easy. Below the senior management levels, officers are by training and conditioning interested in the traditional measures of success of their unit — and those are normally the rate of return on investment capital, sales, costs, and so on. In 1972, R.W. Ackerman found that it took six to eight years to successfully integrate a new social goal into the operations of a firm.[4] The situation may be changing because the managers trained in the late 1960s and early 1970s now have more and more responsibility within corporations, and there is every indication that they have retained many of the social values that were prevalent at that time.[5] However, adjusting to any change, no matter how important and essential it may be, should not be assessed as an easy task. Issuing a directive will not suffice.

Not only is it difficult to make change throughout the operation of the organization, but it is often very difficult to implement new policies with respect to relationships with government at the senior level. Through the years, in many organizations that work regularly with government, a wide variety of contacts are developed with appropriate members of the bureaucracy and it is difficult, and many times unwise, to disturb these arrangements. Any attempt to do so by a newly formed public affairs department that attempts to cut across all lines may indeed fail unless it is done with skill and care, and yet new arrangements may be necessary because of the subtle new changes in the power structure in the government. It is still the view of many CEOs that one-to-one contact is the best way to deal with the government and changing this view, which may or may not be correct depending on the circumstances, is not easy.

Fifth, the public affairs department must have the capacity, responsibility, and authority for briefing anyone approaching the government in any fashion. Government officials are in need of good, solid, factual material and ideas about how to deal with problems. They are totally uninterested in any type of "special pleading" approach that is not associated with a solution to a problem.[6] This need has sometimes been used to argue for the establishment of a public affairs department with depth of expertise in all areas where the firm and the government interrelate, for example, in the economic analysis of trade policy, tax changes, royalty rules, and so forth. While each case must be considered on its merits, there seems to be little reason to duplicate the work of trade associations, line departments, and other areas within the public affairs department. What is important is that information is available and is used effectively.

Sixth, since there is a trend for government officials to meet with organizations representing a number of companies rather than with company officials alone, primarily as a time-saving device and as a method of obtaining, if there is one, a single industry view on an issue, the public affairs department must have the responsibility of advising management on how to work with trade associations and other organizations that can promote the interests of the company in the external environment.

Seventh, the public affairs department must have adequate staff and expertise to be able to recommend, advise, and be involved in choosing the appropriate response to specific situations. How should a firm react to a particular political initiative? Should it ignore it? Should it engage in counter-political activities? If so, what type of tactics should it use? Should it mobilize its employees' and sharehol-ders' support for its position? Should it work with industry groups on a particular issue or go it alone? Should a firm attempt to do some type of social accounting to indicate its contribution to the community within which it operates? If so, how should it be done? Should there be a section on social accounting in the Annual Report? These are examples of the types of questions the department should be capable of answering.

Eighth, the public affairs department must have the responsibility of developing, with senior management, the general strategy of the firm with respect to the external environment. Such a strategy should not be reactive but should be perceptive and based on the probabilities of certain future events occurring. For example, what type of long-term strategy should a firm evolve in face of vague indications of possible threats of nationalization sometime in the future? What actions now will lessen the prospect of threats being converted into reality? What positive actions, if any, should the firm be taking now?

Ninth, and finally, the public affairs department must have the continuing responsibility of determining how the leadership of the firm may make a positive contribution into the determination of the public interest. And the guiding principle must always be, if at all possible, to keep the goals of the firm in reasonable congruence with the goals of society.

Students and practitioners of management who have closely analysed the relationship of business to government argue that one of the greatest problems that management exhibits in its dealings with government is that it does not have any strategy at all. Too often CEOs cannot decide whether or not to respond to a government initiative. By the time they decide they should do something, it is often too late to be effective. Many times firms do not know whether to or how to mount effective political responses. They do not know how to build political constituencies or if they should. In fact, they are often simply inept and incompetent in these areas of vital interest to the corporation.[7]

A properly organized, staffed, and financed public affairs depart-ment should respond to such issues. Whether or not one agrees that in dealing with the political and social environments "we are at the essence of the present challenge facing the very survival of the corporation in to-day's society,"[8] one cannot ignore the reality of the challenge and the need to organize in some systematic manner to deal with it.

Special Interest Groups

Few if any major corporations attempt to deal with government alone. Most, if not all, belong to one or more trade associations and many use other types of organizations, such as professional business-government consulting firms, in order to present their positions. The value and influence of these various organizations differ depending upon the issues in which they are involved and the manner in which they operate. Their role, however, can only be understood within the general context of the significance of special interest groups in the determination and operation of the governmental process.

As the role of government in society has grown, both the difficulty of communicating with government and the need to do so have increased. Consequently, almost every segment of society that has a particular relationship to government is organized to present its views and concepts to the various groups that have some input in determining the laws of the land. While no one seems to know precisely how many "special interest groups" are active in Ottawa, the number is large and seems to be growing. Ken Clements, the Ottawa Chapter President of the Institute of Association Executives, estimated in May of 1980 that there were 300 trade and professional associations in Ottawa who employed over 2,000 people and spent more than $122 million per year.[9]

The range of special interest group organizations is, as to be expected, almost as great as the range of government activities, and the form and structure of organizations is almost as varied. On the one hand, there are groups such as "pro-life" who intensively lobby Members of Parliament one or two times a year and who exert pressure on a member in the way he understands best — by influencing the voters in his constituency; and on the other, there are the permanent, professional organizations that primarily provide technical information to government departments.

Regardless of their form and structure, they all are an integral and legitimate part of the governmental process. If people are going to be deeply affected by legislation, they want to be certain that those responsible for passing that legislation know their views.

Whether such groups are too influential is a matter of great debate, but there is little doubt "the processes of communication that they create are just as important to the resolution of government policy as are those which transmit the wishes of political parties, the opinions of the press, and the advice of permanent officials."[10] In a pluralistic democratic society where a major function of government is to arrange the very different goals of various groups into a consensus made workable by persuasion, the more people that are heard on an issue the better and, presumably, the better any resulting legislation. Whether or not many would go quite so far as some that strong "pressure groups are the essential element of a vigorous democracy" is questionable, but most would agree that "to perform its formidable synthesizing role, [the government] must carry on sustained interaction with every major sector of the national institutional structure, including business, industry, labour, agriculture, religion, education, the mass media, to name only the most obvious. Interest groups may be regarded as the legitimate and rationalized social instruments for carrying on such interactions."[11] Interest groups do have influence and that influence is legitimate. They are an important force in the legislative process in Canada.

It has been argued that by the nature of the political process in play in Canada, "political leaders, including the higher bureaucracy, can and do define and seek the 'public interest' without much need for explanation of their actions or for participation by the general public."[12] However, there is evidence to suggest that special interest groups have always played a role in policy formulation. What is changing is that as the decision-making process becomes more public, the role of interest groups is also becoming more public.

The federal government funds the activities of some associations. In fact, there are those who argue that in a properly functioning pluralistic society, it is incumbent upon the government, within limits, to assist less affluent groups to assure that all views are heard before legislation is enacted.

Given their significance, it is not astonishing that there is an increasing desire by the public and by legislatures to know more about special interest groups — who they represent, how they are financed, and what they are doing. If they have as much influence as alleged then, it is argued, they should be subject to the same type of scrutiny as any other group in the political process. In response to this concern, a movement has developed to require the registration of lobbyists with the Clerks of the Senate and of the House of Commons, and a private member's bill providing "for the registration of lobbyists, and a declaration by them stating in whose interest they are working"[13] was introduced in the Fourth Session of the Thirtieth Parliament by Walter Baker, House Leader of the Official Opposition. The bill imposed a fine and disqualification from lobbying for those convicted of evading the provisions of the legislation. Needless to say, the bill did not go anywhere — private members' bills seldom do — but it is a sign of the changing attitude in Ottawa about the role of special interest groups in the political process. The bill is not, as Baker has pointed out, an indication of disapproval of the work of such groups, but a tacit recognition of their importance and the need to identify more clearly their role in the legislative process.

It is within this context and understanding of the great importance of special interest groups in the formulation of public policy that the role of the business trade associations must be assessed.

Trade Associations: How Useful Are They?

The range of activities and form of organization of business associations is almost as broad as business itself. However, it is possible to make one broad distinction — that is, between associations designed to influence the general direction of national policy and associations organized on a sector basis, whose responsibilities are more directly related to the industries of which they are the representatives. In the first category one may place organizations such as the Business Council on National Issues, the C.D. Howe Research Institute, and the Conference Board in Canada; in the latter, associations such as the Mining Association of Canada and the Canadian Association of Broadcasters. There are overlaps among the activities of the two types, but in general a distinction may be made.

The structure and activities of the Business Council on National Issues (BCNI) clearly illustrates the work of the first type. The BCNI was formed by Letters Patent in March of 1977 by the chief executive officers of 125 major Canadian business firms. It was organized primarily because several leading Canadian executives were concerned about the apparent inability of the Canadian economy to operate with maximum efficiency, the increasing confrontation between and among various segments of society, and the growing worry that the increasing share of the nation's production being handled through government was not an efficient and effective way to assure the highest standard of living for most Canadians. There was a belief that while individual CEOs could always express their individual views, that if there was to be an effective input by business into the policy-making process — into the determination of the public interest — there had to be "co-ordinated presentation of carefully substantiated positive recommendations in readily understood terms."[14]

The BCNI operates through a twenty-three-member policy committee that meets four times a year. This committee chooses the issues to be studied within a general mandate of concentrating on a few specific issues of major concern. The work is carried out by task force members and is supported by well-financed research done by consultants rather than staff. The first major study — one that has received wide approval by the business, academic, and parts of the government community — was on parliamentary reform.[15]

Industry trade associations differ from the general associations in that they are organized primarily along industry lines and normally have much broader functions than the associations that are designed primarily to influence the direction of national policy. The size, structure, and function of such associations are a reflection of the size, structure, and problems of the industries they represent. They range from very large to very small, and they may be organized as federations with provincial and local chapters, or simply unitary bodies in Ottawa. Like all organizations, associations have their problems: if they have a federated structure they have difficulties in getting consensus about issues, but when they are unitary bodies, they are often dominated by one or two large firms.

Most large associations have both a service function and a legislative one. In terms of service to their members, they run seminars, publish magazines and newsletters, operate educational programmes, gather statistics that may be useful to members in their decision making, handle general public relations for the industry, provide market information, and quite often are an instrument for the self-regulation of the industry.

In terms of a legislative function, they promote to all levels of government the views and aspirations of their membership. They monitor, and this is very important, government policies and proposed legislation and communicate the views of their industry, and quite often those of several industries when a consensus is possible, to the appropriate government officials. Top-level association executives pride themselves on being able to predict what the government is likely to do about a particular issue and of having some input into the thinking of the government on the issue. To do this effectively, association executives attempt to establish and maintain close relationships with the key people in the bureaucracy, something that association executives report universally is more difficult to do now than was the case a decade ago primarily because the "old-boy network" type of dealing is past.

The approach of associations is now highly professional and presentations of positions are based more on research than reaction. The fact is "that people of consequence in government have recognized in recent years that they have more problems than they can possibly handle and therefore need useful information and advice from business"[16] or wherever they can get it. Senior government officials' scarcest resource is time and they simply are not interested, except in the most perfunctory of ways, in hearing the traditional lobbyist's pitch, but they do need and welcome information. As one association executive put it, "in Ottawa, there is little natural opportunity for cross-pollination of ideas between business and the civil service, and for this reason alone, trade associations in Ottawa have a monumental and never-ending task of trying to explain the business perception of the world to an intelligent, but nevertheless isolated, bureaucracy."

One particularly influential trade association leader has written that to be successful in presenting a position, it is best to be representing a large number of voters, be allied with significant groups (in Canada, alliances with farmers, fishermen, and labour seem to help), not call for the expenditure of government funds, add to total employment, be in tune with the political climate of the moment, have useful and accurate information about the impact of the issue, be supported by other trade associations, and be contacting the right people, that is, the people with input at all levels of the decision-making process, at the right time, that is, before there is legislation before Parliament.[17]

For effective action, timing and people are critical. As one executive of a major trade association stated, "under the parliamentary system, once the minister is convinced by his bureaucrats that action is necessary, and he persuades his Cabinet colleagues of this, by the time a bill clears caucus, and is tabled, it is often game over. . . ."[18]

Leaders of associations feel that it is imperative that the CEOs of the firms in the industry support associations not only through financing, but through activity. Indeed, without strong participation by CEOs on their boards, associations feel that their capacity to influence policy is weak. Moreover, unlike most CEOs, trade association executives feel that approaches to senior public servants and ministers by associations with well-thought-out positions and mature, politically sensitive advice are far more effective than individual approaches by CEOs.

There is a general view that the ritual appearance of the representatives of the large associations before a segment of the Cabinet, while likely to remain as one of the institutions of our time, is essentially ineffective in any meaningful manner. There are many who do not take such groups seriously. "If the Chamber has ever had a president whose political philosophy was not well to the right of Louis XVI, then he has been remarkably successful in concealing it . . . such organizations who reiterate such completely predictable views *ad nauseam* simply lose much of their credibility with the upper echelons of the government . . ."[19] is the way one politician put it, but it should be noted that senior economic ministers report such meetings, while predictable, are useful.

Knowing the system, providing quality information, getting consensus, structuring ongoing relationships, professional approaches, providing continuity of views, monitoring the decision-making process — this is what the legislative side of the trade association business in Canada is all about. And few would disagree with the conclusion of one association executive that "our network of pressure groups presents a sensitive device for monitoring public performance, and can contribute immensely to the smooth integration of our political and social systems."

Perhaps Darcy McKeough, former member of the government of Ontario, stated it most directly when he compared the advice of two different politicians on how to influence government. "One was the new federal Minister of Public Works. He said, 'Of course government listens to lobbyists — that's the way the system works'. The other politician . . . advised a group of truckers to ring Queen's Park with their trucks in a protest against government transportation policy. The first politician spoke the truth . . . he invited citizens to present their views and he said they will be listened to. It sounds like an intelligent approach to public policy formation. The second politician's assumption that brute force and tying up of the public streets will somehow appeal to the better instincts of Ontario politicians, or lead them logically to a favourable conclusion, is stupid and self-defeating. It is an insult to the intelligence of all concerned."[20]

The amount of association input into the policy process depends upon the issue. Some associations have major, almost daily, interchange with departments on regulations and tax matters; at other times they may be concerned about proposed legislation and therefore involved in making the industries' views known within the department and to the people who are preparing the first memorandum to Cabinet about the matter. As the preparation of legislation goes forward, there may be contact with senior members of the department, then, if necessary, the responsible Cabinet minister. If legislation is being introduced, it may be important to discuss the matter with Members of Parliament who are members of the government, and even with members of the opposition. If a bill is referred to committee, appearances may be made before the committee on various aspects of the bill. In short, there are an incredible number of places where input may be made and they all must be monitored and assessed in terms of their value. What that may be depends a great deal on the nature of the legislation and the significance it has to the industry.

Approaches to the various players in the process may be made directly in personal or written communication or by brief before a group or committee. During the entire process it may be significant to keep the media informed of what is going on, and in some circumstances it may even be valuable to implement some type of campaign among the voters in various members' constituencies.

Who is approached and how they are approached obviously depends on the circumstances. Robert Presthus, in his extensive study of special interest groups, found that they themselves ranked the bureaucracy as the most important group to approach, twice as important as the next group, legislators, who were ranked slightly ahead of Cabinet members and almost six times as important as House of Commons committees in terms of significance in the formulation of legislation.[21]

Everyone can get access to the traditional bureaucracy, but Presthus found that businessmen had, by a very small margin, the most access, whereas representatives of agriculture and education had the greatest access to the members of the Cabinet.[22] Again, it is worth noting that the bureaucracy at the department level uses and interfaces with associations because of the information that they can supply. Sometimes it is technical knowledge about the impact of a piece of legislation, sometimes it is reaction about the political acceptability of a proposal, and so on. In any event the contacts are frequent and important, and presumably of some use to both parties.

Officials of the Prime Minister's Office (PMO), as to be expected, relate to outside groups continuously and actively, but other central agencies of government do not. The Federal-Provincial Relations Office (FPRO) has little contact with outside organizations, and the Privy Council Office (PCO) perhaps even less. The fact is that officers in those branches of government "simply do not believe that interest groups play a significant role in the policy arena, possibly because groups do not come to them or they avoid groups . . . PCO officials tend to be self-sufficient and, therefore, somewhat closed to such interactions . . .,"[23] and yet some would argue that it is within these agencies that the major policy decisions of government can be most directly influenced by permanent officials.

The effectiveness of access depends upon the legitimacy of associations and the power of the groups to which they have access. In this respect it is clear that the easiest access is probably to M.P.'s and it is with the M.P.'s that special interest groups appear to have their greatest legitimacy[24] — primarily because it is generally recognized that association members and officers can give an M.P. a reading of the political pros and cons of a specific piece of legislation, often for the member's own constituency — and it is the back-bencher and opposition M.P.'s who are usually most sensitive to direct public concern about legislation.

Time spent by associations with opposition members and back-benchers is more often than not an investment in the future. Parties occasionally do change positions, back-benchers do become Cabinet ministers — even leaders of parties — and so it is wise for associations to cultivate these people. However, given the fact that M.P.'s do not have much influence on the evolution and development of policy, the high rate of legitimacy and impact that associations have with M.P.'s should not be considered very significant — at least not very important in terms of actual shaping of legislation.

The same is true with respect to House of Commons committees. While associations and their members appear before committees with some frequency, one can almost conclude that such appearances are more for form than substance. There is almost universal agreement that House committees, as they now operate, have little relevance to the basic legislation that is enacted by Parliament.[25]

All legislation must be passed by the Senate, so it is possible upon occasion for a particularly controversial bill to be held up in committees of the Senate — almost always with the government's knowledge and often with its support. Consequently, there are occasions when the Senate may be useful to a trade association in putting forth a particular position, but while it often provides a forum for the dissemination of particular views about legislation, it must be recognized that the Senate's influence is practically non-existent.[26]

Because of the high degree of Cabinet secrecy — until 1979 it was impossible to find out which Cabinet members served on which committees — it is difficult to appraise the impact of trade associations on Cabinet members. The results of a survey of 20 former Cabinet members suggests that it varies widely. On balance, as a former finance minister put it, "large groups are treated seriously because government clearly does not want to antagonize a major group ... moreover, they can provide important special technical information," or as another reported, "the input on technical questions is invaluable." On the other hand, there are ministers who found dealings with associations "difficult and unproductive." A few in fact stated that while they would always meet with associations, they would not discuss final points with them — but only principles, "since too often associations had to present consensus views that were well-watered down." Interestingly enough, one former Cabinet member reported that he found the associations more useful to him when he was in opposition than when in government simply because they provided him with ammunition for question period in the House of Commons.[27]

Obviously, one cannot generalize from observations of Cabinet members representing different areas of the country and involved with different portfolios. What can be said, however, is that associations have access to ministers, are listened to, and probably have somewhat less influence and acceptability among Cabinet members than among Members of Parliament.

Chief executive officers reported a wide range of time spent with general organizations such as the BCNI — from zero to as high as 20 per cent with the modal amount being 1 per cent — and, as to be expected, there was a wide range of opinions about the effectiveness of such organizations. A few believed that they did little good, but 20 per cent reported that they thought they were very effective, 50 per cent thought that they were moderately effective, and about 25 per cent thought that they were not as effective as they should be. As some CEOs stated, such organizations are "more effective than I think we realize, but less than we like although it does seem to be getting better" or "I am not sure how effective they are, but I believe they have a potential for being useful . . ." and "certainly greater influence than associations that consistently adopt a negative attitude to government legislative proposals."

Another group believed that the impact of such groups as the BCNI is "limited . . . in part because of the adversary approach that has developed between business and civil servants and some politicians . . ." and that they are "good at influencing government policy, but weak at changing policy. . . ." Finally, there are those who believed that such groups are simply ineffective. As one CEO stated, "none are effective . . .," "too confrontational — not very useful. . . ."

Cabinet ministers, on the other hand, found the research reports of such organizations particularly helpful. Former Ministers of Finance all reported that the studies of the Conference Board and the C.D. Howe Institute influenced their thinking and provided useful countervailing material to that presented by traditional departmental and other sources. Indeed, in the policy departments, there is no question that such reports and studies are significant.

But influencing and actually changing views are different things. While one CEO reported that "organizations of any type, I think, are less effective in their dealings with government than are individuals," the development of the BCNI was tacit recognition that the days of the strong interrelationship between senior ministers and businessmen and senior mandarins and businessmen are over — over not only because of the change in the players or because many of the persons involved want it to be over, but because the system of decision making in Ottawa has changed so the one-to-one relationship is no longer as effective as it once was. Indeed, it is much less easy for the businessman, or indeed anyone else, to identify the players with power, and when they can be identified they are not easily approached, and when approached they may not have a great deal of sympathy for the underlying philosophy inherent in the approach — that is, greater reliance on the private sector for the operation of the economy — of organizations like the BCNI.

How do CEOs evaluate the success of trade associations? The answer depends on what they are perceived as doing. In terms of changing the direction of general national policy, CEOs do not think associations are very significant. As one put it, "I have many concerns about the traditional trade associations with respect to their influence on national policies . . . on so many occasions they find it very difficult to achieve a consensus among their members and any consensus is so seriously watered down, that it can hardly be deemed to be an effective policy statement. . . ." However, on specific representational matters they are perceived as being important and effective by more than 60 per cent of the CEOs. As one stated, "trade associations are effective when they deal with a limited, usually technical problem. . . ."

It is an appropriate generalization that CEOs do not see the traditional trade associations, important and significant as they are in the policy process, as the instrument for changing the general direction of policy in the nation. In general, conclusions about their effectiveness seem to some degree to be in the "eye of the beholder." W.T. Stanbury believes that the work of the trade associations with respect to the Competition Act, the Patent Law Revisions, and the Borrowers and Depositors Protection Act is evidence of the success of the business lobby; Alasdair McKichan considers the history of this same legislation as evidence of its failure.[28]

What then is the reality? The fact is that associations are important and that they play a significant role. The changing nature of the policy-making process in Ottawa plus the sheer complexity of government has meant that their influence is less than it perhaps once was on general policy issues, but on development of specific parts of legislation, regulations, and tax rulings, the associations play an important role. Their current difficulties, if they may be called that, arise from the fact that they have less contact with the significant players in the central agencies such as the PCO, than they have in the traditional departments, and yet it is in the PCO and PMO where many broad policy concepts are gestated. On the other hand, their influence and legitimacy with the legislative branch of government is high, and if this arm of the democratic process becomes stronger, as it probably will, associations will play a more significant role in the next decade than they have in the past.

Associations have influence, but they do not in and by themselves have power. The degree to which they can exert influence on the decision makers and assist them in the governmental process will always have to be the measure of their success.[29]

Public Affairs Consulting Companies

With the increasing size of government and the almost constant interaction of government with business, it is not surprising that in addition to the increase in size and professionalism of trade associations, there has been a growth in the number of professional public affairs consulting firms that assist business in its contacts with government.

While such firms vary in degree, they all basically do the same things. In the words of one major company president, "we attempt to keep a client informed about current and probable public policy matters, both of a general nature, and those specific to its interests"[30] — in short, they provide an early-warning system to their clients about forthcoming government policies. In addition, many firms will work with a company in developing a policy for dealing with government; however, most do not commit to provide access to key governmental personnel although they are, of course, identified for the client. They help corporations plan responses to particular situations and may brief executives for appearances before regulatory bodies and parliamentary committees. Indeed, anything that government does or may do that impinges on the activity of their clients is basically within the terms of reference of such firms. As Thomas d'Aquino, President of Intercounsel, stated in a letter to the members of the Business Council on National Issues, "we assist senior management in three principal ways: first, in grasping quickly the significance and potential impact of problems and policy issues, in particular in their formative stage; second, in planning initiatives and shaping effective responses to situations created by particular government policies, legislation, directives, and regulations; third, in understanding the complex structure and process of government as they evolve under the influence of rapidly shifting political events, subtle turns in ideology, organizational developments, and changing personalities."

How do CEOs perceive and use such firms? Twenty per cent of all CEOs have in fact at one time or another employed such an organization. Those that do find that "they are valuable for information purposes," "that they can save you time." The CEOs who do not use these firms by and large do not have any specific reason for not using them other than that they have not found their services essential in the conduct of business. Some specifically reject their use, because "we are generally successful in Ottawa with a one-on-one basis with ministers and senior officials. They listen to us as long as we are well prepared and know what we are taking about" or "we do not use professional business-government consulting firms since we made the decision to create a position of public affairs executive within the company" or "we feel that our own people are our best resource" and "we don't think they can help us much."

In short, public business-government affairs firms offer a service that management can and does use, but they are not perceived by senior executives as an effective instrument in helping to change the general thrust of national policy — and neither do the firms see themselves as playing such a role.

Staff and Other Approaches

A small number of large corporations handle the day-to-day relations with the government by maintaining a permanent staff of employees in Ottawa. For those who do, such people are expected to achieve, as one executive explained, "a complete understanding of the system, a working or at least a communicating relationship on at least three levels of administration, and an understanding on a day-to-day basis

of the principal concerns of the various departments of government."
The group in almost all cases is responsible for liaison with government departments and for monitoring and interpreting legislation.
Obtaining information is also an important function of some Ottawa offices.

For those firms who do not maintain an Ottawa office, the reasons vary, although the most important seems to be that they can use their trade associations as listening posts and information sources. They also stress that the CEO has the major responsibility for business-government relations and it is important to have his staff for this function in the corporate office. As one stated, "the blood of the bureaucracy is very thick . . . and if anyone is in Ottawa too long with the same group . . . he becomes co-opted . . . he knows what is going on in Ottawa, but he may not know what is happening to the country. . . ."

In other words, firms that have offices in Ottawa by and large perceive the function of those offices as providing staff support, very much in the same way as they view the government-business professional relations firms as providing staff assistance, on specific issues. They do not in any sense use them as centres for the development of general strategy and policy with respect to the overall response of the corporation to government initiatives.

There are many other professionals that corporations use in dealing with government. Probably the most important are the major law firms. Presthus found that "40 per cent of all groups, led by business, social-recreational, and professional groups, have at one time or another employed a lobbyist or a lawyer to represent them."[31] Andrew Roman is explicit about the role played by lawyers when he writes that "C-256 [The Competition Act] . . . would provide a full-employment programme for the Canadian lobbying industry including a large number of members of the legal profession. . . . Some of the country's most senior lawyers made speeches containing a litany of hypothetical horrors about the bill. . . ."[32]

There is little exact knowledge about the role played by lawyers, but given the fact that so many have political experience — the House of Commons and the Cabinet are dominated by them — it is not astonishing that when they return to their law practices, they are solicited to give advice on how to deal with government.

With the growing complexity of the relationship between business and government, the use of accountants and consultants of all types has become not only a practice but a necessity for the corporation with extensive dealings with government. At what point these professionals are lobbyists is almost impossible to identify and perhaps, really, is not of much importance.

Many CEOs still firmly believe that the best approach to government is on a one-to-one meeting with decision makers, and some CEOs have developed great skill in dealing with government officials, Members of Parliament, and Cabinet members. Those that do it best work at it constantly, are exceedingly well prepared, and have specific requests. Moreover, they normally spread their efforts over a wide range of people so they become well known among all groups: M.P.'s, bureaucracy, Cabinet. In many instances, the people contacted are not directly involved and indeed may not have any impact on the decision-making process, but an aura is created around a project that becomes part of the *ambiance* within which decisions are made, and the value of this is incalculable.[33]

Do Tactical Capabilities Create the Strategies?

The advice to CEOs about dealing with government that emanates from the heads of trade associations, business-government professional firms, and other observers of the relationship is almost all the same, and quite clear. In order to work well with government, it is important that a corporation have available (1) someone who understands how the system of government works — where the decisions are made; (2) an early-warning system about the type of legislation that is being proposed or the general direction of regulations; (3) knowledge of who the key decision makers in the system actually are — not who may be in fact occupying a particular position but who actually has influence or power; (4) good rapport with influential people at whatever level of the bureaucracy they may be in; (5) capacity, once a problem area is identified, to enlist allies to the cause; (6) ability to present a position to the appropriate people, for as one expert put it, "there is often the tendency to look too high for decision makers and to think that ministers make all decisions . . . it is a waste to be in the wrong place at the wrong time . . . and worse, genuine ignorance on industry's part might be construed as a political end-run by the people you really should be seeing;"[34] and (7) understanding of other pressures that governments must face and consideration of them when offering a solution to government. Finally, it is always suggested that business relations with government cannot be better than business relations with the press.

The advice is unquestionably correct: business can relate more effectively with government if there is more understanding of the system, more commitment of resources, better public relations, and more effective work with the media.

Such a strategy presupposes an issue-by-issue approach to government-business relations. It helps business to understand each piece of legislation that may influence its activities, and it assumes that if each issue is dealt with effectively, the consequences will be the optimum relationship between the public and the private sector and the fulfilment of the public interest. It is, essentially, a strategy of accommodation; and while this in the Canadian context may have been the most appropriate approach in the past, it is far from certain that it may be the best in the future. The reality is that the strategy has not been effective in lessening business-government tension, in bringing about a strong economic performance in Canada, or in lessening the role of government in society.

It is apparent that the issue-by-issue approach has dominated business-government relations, not because CEOs believed that it was successful in fulfilling their objectives, but because it was almost mandated by the tactics and tools that business had to use in dealing with government. Clearly, important as the issue-by-issue strategy may be, it is not in and by itself achieving the results that the private sector must obtain if the interrelationship between business and government is to be more satisfactory in the decades ahead than it has been in the immediate past.

Notes

[1] H. Igor Ansoff, "The Changing Shape of the Strategic Problem," in *Strategic Management: A New View of Business Policy and Planning*, edited by Dan E. Schendel and Charles W. Hofer (Boston: Little, Brown, 1979), pp. 35–40.

[2] For a discussion of various approaches to managing and implementing public affairs programmes, see Phyllis S. McGrath, *Action Plans for Public Affairs*, Report No. 733 (New York: Conference Board, 1977).

[3] See Chapter 3.

[4] Robert W. Ackerman, "How Companies Respond to Social Demands," *Harvard Business Review* 51 (July-August 1973): 88–98.

[5] Ramon J. Aldag and Donald W. Jackson Jr., "Assessment of Attitudes Toward Social Responsibilities," *Journal of Business Administration* 8 (Spring 1977), pp. 69–70. ". . . the findings relating to age and years of business experience imply that while increased exposure to the business world may lead to attitudes which are more favourable to business in regard to governmental restraints, reallocation of corporate resources, and adequacy of corporate social efforts, it does not necessarily lead either to an increased emphasis on the goal of profit maximization or to a distaste for social actions."

[6] Andrew Kniewasser, "How Do You Communicate With Government," Speech delivered to the annual convention of the Ontario Chamber of Commerce, Toronto, 13 May 1980, p. 2.

[7] Donald H. Thain, "The Mistakes of Business in Dealing with Politics and Government," *Business Quarterly* 44 (Autumn 1979): 46–54.

[8] J. Duncan Edmonds, "The Public Affairs Function in Canadian Corporations," (Ottawa: JDE Consulting Services, 1975).

[9] Robert Stevens, "Lobbyists a Big Cog in Ottawa Economy," *The Ottawa Journal* (8 May 1980), p. 29.

[10] A. Paul Pross, "Canadian Pressure Groups in the 1970s: Their Role and Their Relations with the Public Service," *Canadian Public Administration* 18 (Spring 1975), p. 122. The rise of the very powerful one-issue special interest groups has become a matter of great concern to many legislators. It is of particular significance in the

United States where in the late 1970s members of the Congress were defeated by groups on one issue, and one issue alone. Particularly powerful have been the "pro-life" anti-abortion on demand organizations and the anti-gun control lobbyists.

11 Robert Presthus, *Elite Accommodation in Canadian Politics* (Toronto: Macmillan, 1973), p. 143.

12 Robert Presthus, "Interest Groups and the Canadian Parliament: Activities, Interaction, Legitimacy, and Influence," *Canadian Journal of Political Science* 4 (December 1971), p. 446.

13 Canada, Parliament, House of Commons, *An Act to Register Lobbyists*, Bill C-255, Fourth Session, Thirtieth Parliament, 30 October 1978.

14 W.D. Archbold, "Business Council on National Issues: A New Factor in Business Communication," *The Canadian Business Review* 4 (Summer 1977), p. 13.

15 Thomas d'Aquino, G. Bruce Doern, and Cassandra Blair, *Parliamentary Government in Canada: A Critical Assessment and Suggestions for Change*, study prepared for the Business Council on National Issues (Ottawa: Intercounsel Limited, 1979).

16 Kniewasser, *op. cit.*, p. 1.

17 Alasdair J. McKichan, "Comments" on W.T. Stanbury, "Lobbying and Interest Group Representation in the Legislative Process," in *The Legislative Process in Canada: The Need for Reform*, edited by W.A.W. Neilson and J.C. MacPherson (Montreal: The Institute for Research on Public Policy, 1978), pp. 219–24.

18 See Appendix A for source of trade association comments.

19 John M. Godfrey, "Introductory Remarks" for panel on *How to Deal Effectively with Governments* (Montebello: Institute of Canadian Advertising, September 1972).

20 W. Darcy McKeough, Remarks delivered to the Young Presidents' Organization, London, Ontario, 6 May 1980.

21 Presthus, *Elite Accommodation in Canadian Politics*, *op. cit.*, p. 153.

22 *Ibid.*, pp. 144–56.

23 Colin Campbell and George J. Szablowski, *The Superbureaucrats: Structure and Behaviour in Central Agencies* (Toronto: Macmillan, 1979), pp. 201, 203.

24 Presthus, "Interest Groups and the Canadian Parliament: Activities, Interaction, Legitimacy, and Influence," *op. cit.*, p. 454.

25 See d'Aquino *et al.*, *op. cit.*, and R.M. MacIntosh, "The Role of Business in Public Policy," Remarks delivered to the Institute of Management Consultants of Ontario, Toronto, 14 May 1979, p. 9.

26 Andrew Roman, "Comments" on W.T. Stanbury, "Lobbying and Interest Group Representation in the Legislative Process," in *The Legislative Process in Canada: The Need for Reform*, edited by W.A.W. Neilson and J.C. MacPherson (Montreal: The Institute for Research on Public Policy, 1978), pp. 208–12. Roman has a wide definition of lobbyist — indeed anyone who has any interest whatsoever in legislation. He includes on his list law firms and lawyers, party bagmen, senators, and M.P.'s, professional full-time lobbying firms who represent clients, and employees of major firms. To be consistent, presumably he should also include the minister introducing the bill, the department, and anyone, such as special assistants to the minister, who might have been associated with the legislation being considered.

27 Of twenty former federal Cabinet ministers, half said they had no influence. In the traditional economic portfolios the impact was the greatest.

28 McKichan, *op. cit.*, pp. 221–22.

[29] The Canadian Federation of Independent Businessmen, which has organized a system whereby individual Members of Parliament are contacted directly by constituents, is probably the single most influential association in Canada with the legislature. In turn, M.P.'s can and do influence Cabinet members and other decision makers, and as their power grows, so will the power of groups such as the CFIB.

[30] William M. Lee, *A Profile of Executive Consultants Limited* (Ottawa: Executive Consultants Ltd., 1980), p. 2.

[31] Presthus, *Elite Accommodation in Canadian Politics*, *op. cit.*, p. 168.

[32] Roman, *op. cit.*, pp. 208–9.

[33] Probably the best example of this type of activity was the work done by Robert Blair before the Alaska Pipeline decision, and the continuous work of Jack Gallagher for tax allowances in the development of North Sea gas and oil.

[34] W.H. Nevillle, Comments delivered to the fall meeting of the Canadian Chemical Producers Association, Ottawa, 1979.

Decision Making in the Executive Branch of Government

6

As leaders of a significant sector of society, chief executive officers have the responsibility, indeed the necessity, of relating to the government at two very different and distinct levels. First, under the "consent doctrine," they have the obligation of making an input into the determination of public policy; and, second, once the public interest is established, as expressed by the laws of the land, they must operate their organizations in conformity with both the reality and the spirit of the law. In order to fulfil these responsibilities they, or their chief advisers, must know how public policy is made and who makes it. Unfortunately, such knowledge is not always readily attainable for while the government process, in a formal sense, is well understood, an understanding of form does not guarantee an understanding of reality. For example, is policy established by political parties at their political conventions? Or is it determined by Members of Parliament? Or by the executive branch of government: the Prime Minister and his Cabinet? Or is policy actually determined by the members of the public service who advise on and administer policy? The answer is that all these groups play a part, and therefore if one hopes to influence the formulation of policy, one must interact with each of them. The problem is, however, that the role and power of each group in the process change constantly and consequently the impact that must be made on each also changes. And, indeed, the set of forces that called for the formulation of any particular policy in the first place may be changed by some external event that makes the entire exercise redundant.

Because of the difficulties in identifying and explaining the public policy decision-making process, there is a view that no one is really responsible for policy — that somehow decisions happen almost by accident. It is alleged "that no one really runs the Government of Canada. The Government of Canada is not a machine, which can be run, but a series of discrete, random events; a happening. . . . There are so many levels in the hierarchy, and so many events interacting with one another, that the government is beyond the effective control of anyone at any particular point in time."[1] But surely this analysis is incorrect. The government of Canada in many ways is a machine. It is an organization that is managed. Important decisions are made by people conscious of the fact that they are making decisions, who act after weighing the various inputs from the different groups affected by a decision. To conclude otherwise is to assert that democracies are not governable — a patently false concept, since they are governed every day.

No one would deny, however, that policy making is very complex, and despite all of the studies that have been made about the way in which government decides, if one accepts the definition of theory that it has the specific task of providing "a system of generalizations that can be used to make correct predictions about the consequences of any change in circumstances . . . [and] . . . its performance is to be judged by the precision, scope, and conformity with experience of the predictions it yields,"[2] then one has to conclude that we do not have adequate theories to explain the way in which public policy decisions are made.

Although there are no general theories of policy making that are particularly useful to the CEO in developing a strategy for dealing with government, there have been a great number of studies that explain (theorize about?) the way specific policies are developed, and there has been some attempt to make certain generalizations about specific aspects of public policy making, for example, the role of the public service in determining policy. Some studies are prescriptive — how policy ought to be made; some are analytical — how it is actually done; and some are organizational — how policy making should be examined in order to determine precisely when and where and by whom policies were created. There are, it seems, an almost infinite variety and combination of these approaches, and anyone who wants to understand how decisions are made by governments is well advised to study these analyses of decision making in specific situations.[3]

The common thread that runs through most studies of policy making is that the goals, aspirations, philosophies, and views of the persons making the decision on the appropriate role of the state in society have a very large impact on the nature of the decision that is made. The fact that in many public policy areas there are no objective performance standards against which to measure results, for example, rate of return on capital invested, means that there is far more opportunity for the decision maker to bring his own personal views to play in making decisions than is the case in business. If you want to know the probable thrust of any particular decision, you have to know who the decision makers are, and know them well.

The degree of power and influence that any individual has in the decision-making process is very much determined by the position he holds in the institutional or organizational structure that is established for making decisions. Again, this seems obvious, but the structure for making policy has changed dramatically in the past few years, and while it may not have reduced the power and influence of individuals, *per se*, the change has meant that the power and influence held by a person by virtue of the position that he holds has changed significantly. For example, the power and influence of the bureaucrats in the Department of Finance, and indeed of the Minister of Finance, has been diminished substantially over the past decade by the creation of new departments to deal with specific economic problems, such as Regional Economic Expansion. No Minister of Finance, regardless of how powerful and popular he may be, will ever have the power that Ministers of Finance held before the reorganization.

It is accepted as a truism that Canada is governed — policy was made — until the late 1960s in a very pragmatic manner by strong, independent Cabinet ministers supported by very strong and capable deputies. In the 1970s, this system of governing was changed by the development of an administrative system that tried to assure that decisions throughout the government were made in a related, integrated manner. While one of the results of the new system has been a decline in the power of individual ministers and deputies, it has led to an increase in the influence and power of other members of the executive. In politics as in physics, there is no such thing as a vacuum, and as power has declined in one area, it has increased in another. There is still as much decision making on the significant issues of policy from the top down as there ever was — perhaps more.

As the organizational structure continues to change, the locus of power and influence will also change, and a knowledge of such changes is fundamental to any understanding of the policy-making process in Canada. This is not to argue that knowing the characteristics of the decision makers and the nature of the system in which they operate is in and by itself sufficient for an understanding of the development of any specific policy — the myriad of other forces that impact on decision making such as the press, public opinion, interest groups, acts of God, and everything else have to be considered — but it is to contend that a basic understanding of these factors is a necessary condition for any comprehension of the broad policy-making processes in government.

The Cabinet Is Not What It Used To Be

The most significant development in the decision-making process in Ottawa in the post–World War II period has been the major change in the way in which the Cabinet — the single most important power centre with respect to policy in the government — operates. Because it has changed, there has been a dramatic alteration in the location of influence and power in the bureaucracy, and these changes have altered the relation of the government, in a great many ways, to the people it governs.

Historically, the Cabinet worked in a very private fashion. In fact in the early administrations of Mackenzie King, there were no agendas for meetings, no minutes were kept, and no officials attended. In many ways the Cabinet was the fiefdom of the Prime Minister who operated it to suit his personal predilections. As government became more complex, during World War II, the Prime Minister occasionally established Cabinet committees to deal with specific problems, but it was on a very *ad hoc* basis and committees had no power to make any type of decision. They simply served as vehicles for permitting more extensive discussion of particular situations.

Under such a system of administration, there was very little co-ordination among departments and very little effort to relate policies in one area with those in another. Any interrelationship that was required was handled through informal channels. Individual ministers accepted the responsibility and assumed the authority for developing policies in their areas and administering their departments. Strong ministers such as Howe, Gardiner, Claxton, and Martin ran their departments in their own way without much advice, let alone interference from their colleagues. The principle of Cabinet collective responsibility was based on the commonsense notion of confidence in one's colleagues, rather than on the concept of sharing of knowledge and decision making.

It was traditional, in those less complex times, for ministers to stay in a portfolio for some time and for them to relate throughout the country with the interests most concerned about the impact of policies that they proposed. Ministers such as C.D. Howe worked with the entire business community on a continuous and informal basis. Indeed, Howe had no doubts about how the country should be run, and "through [his] unpretentious offices in Number One Temporary Building passed lines of economic control that stretched from Halifax to Victoria, from the Newfoundland fishery to the aluminum smelter at Kitimat (being constructed in 1952 at a cost of $350 million), and from the auto parts factories of St. Catharines to the uranium mines of Great Bear Lake. Every day, over the phone, by letter and in person, Howe was informed of what was happening or what was about to happen everywhere in Canada. . . . Howe was, in short, the leader of a national business community as well as a party leader and a minister of the crown."[4] Moreover, during the war a great many of the men who eventually assumed positions of responsibility and authority within the private sector worked with Howe, so the relationship was personal as well as professional. When a CEO wanted to have an input into the formulation of policy, he knew precisely with whom to talk — and he was always certain of a warm reception because the view of the minister about the role of government in the economy was very close to his own.

In order to carry out their responsibilities, Howe and the other ministers surrounded themselves with strong deputies who quickly learned to operate in the direct fashion of their ministers. As Gardiner, Howe, Abbot, Claxton, and Martin dominated the Cabinet, their deputies — an incredibly able group (possibly one of the finest teams of public servants ever assembled) — through their ability and influence dominated the public service. In the way that the ministers developed a large network of friends throughout the country, so did the deputies. Interaction between government and various sectors of society was quick, friendly, and often on a personal basis. The Canadian pre-war tradition, adapted from the British, of a strong team of deputies working together relatively anonymously, to administer the government and to advise discretely on the formulation of policy, continued into the early 1960s. And partly because the tasks of the government were less complex, partly because the senior people knew each other and had worked together for years, partly because those in power selected those who would work with them (and, of course, they selected people in their own mould), the system was reasonably effective.

When John Diefenbaker was elected in 1957, some of the problems with this rather informal, personal, non-co-ordinated system became apparent — problems that would have surfaced within a few years even if the government had not changed. The difficulties in Mr. Diefenbaker's administration did not arise because the senior public service was political in the narrow sense of the term — although most of the senior public servants had served only under a Liberal administration[5] — but rather because the prevailing *ad hoc* system had no way of adjusting to new people, to new ideas, or to new management methods. And it was not capable of bringing about the co-ordination that the incredible rate of growth in scope and volume of government activities required.

Lester Pearson faced the same difficulties when he became Prime Minister. As a consequence of an inadequate administrative structure, the governments in the late 1950s and in the 1960s could generate neither for themselves nor for the public a clear idea of what they were trying to do. In a very real sense, policy making was disorganized and chaotic.

Except for the Treasury Board, there is no constitutional or legislative provision for the establishment of committees of Cabinet. However, during the early years of his administration, Mr. Pearson, in an effort to cope with the increasing load of government activity, began appointing *ad hoc* committees of Cabinet to deal with specific problems. Such committees were always used to consider individual policy issues and had no authority to make any decisions. That power was kept in the Cabinet. Committees themselves initiated nothing and decided nothing. However, as the work-load of the Cabinet increased and more and more issues needed more detailed examination, particularly because so many matters involved more than one department, Mr. Pearson finally put into place a formal Cabinet committee structure.[6] Indeed, by the end of his administration, he had created nine standing committees, three of which he chaired himself, that had referred to them from Cabinet automatically all matters within their jurisdiction. With the establishment in 1968 of the Committee on Priorities and Planning, because of a "serious need of a systematic assessment of over-all priorities and expenditures"[7] by a more cohesive body than the Cabinet, the movement to the committee system of government was almost complete. The day of the independent strong minister and department was to all intents and purposes over. No minister, however powerful and politically popular, could any longer operate in the independent way ministers had functioned in the 1950s and early 1960s.

The election of Pierre Trudeau further strengthened the Cabinet committee system. As has often been pointed out, Mr. Trudeau's approach to politics and government is rational, pragmatic, and orderly.[8] In many way he may be considered the ultimate bureaucrat — he insists on a thorough study of all alternatives based on all possible facts before making any decision. He was, at the beginning of his Prime Ministership, determined to have in place as soon as possible a system of policy making wherein (1) ministers consulted with each other about interrelated matters, (2) there was co-ordination, (3) there was collective responsibility for Cabinet decisions, in fact as well as in perception and constitutional necessity, and (4) ministers — as the elected representatives of the people — had more influence (they always had more power) than officials on the ultimate choice of a course of action. He wanted his ministers to use a rational approach to decision making — an approach based on a clear-cut set of options determined after a thorough study of alternatives related to a predetermined set of priorities.

In an attempt to achieve these goals, Mr. Trudeau made the Cabinet committee system an integral part of the policy-making process. Whereas in all previous administrations, matters went to the Cabinet and were then referred to the appropriate committee, under Mr. Trudeau items went to the appropriate committee of the Cabinet before they went to the full Cabinet. The most important committee by far was still the Committee on Priorities and Planning, which he as Prime Minister chaired and which was apparently made up of the more senior ministers. The task of the committee was to set the tone and the thrust of the government by establishing priorities, initiating reorganization of departments, establishing special studies and commissions, and in short determining the agenda for government action. It was the only committee of Cabinet that was closed — any Cabinet member could attend any other committee any time he or she wished (with the exception of those dealing with security matters). In order to be certain that every minister was informed of what was going on in every committee, the agenda of all committees was circulated to all members of the Cabinet.

When Joe Clark became Prime Minister, the search continued for more effective means of establishing policies and making decisions. Influenced by the view that much of government administration and policy determination was associated with the resolution of conflict, Mr. Clark attempted to move as much of the reconciliation of different views as far as possible down in the system. There was a general belief that the Cabinet was too large a body for effective decision making and that too many matters that took too much time still came to the Cabinet for consideration. Consequently, Mr. Clark organized an Inner Cabinet, which took over the work of the Priorities and Planning Committee. It was responsible for setting the general thrust of the government, approving the broad work programmes of the Cabinet committees, approving the fiscal stance of the government, and allocating resources to the major policy areas in the various Cabinet committees. However, unlike the Priorities and Planning Committee of Mr. Trudeau, the Inner Cabinet had final decision-making authority, and once it had decided, decisions were reported to the full Cabinet for information purposes only. The Inner Cabinet was not established to referee disputes in Cabinet committees, which were expected to come to their own conclusions, but rather to deal with very specific matters. Decisions of the Inner Cabinet could not be re-opened except by agreement of the Prime Minister who, of course, chaired the Cabinet and the Inner Cabinet.

There was much press discussion about the formation of an Inner Cabinet — not so much about what it did but about how it was perceived by ministers who were not members. As is generally the case in such situations, the public did not have strong views about the matter and members of the government strongly supported the concept. In fact, there were few complaints from ministers who were not members of the Inner Cabinet because (1) if there was an issue that was of extreme importance to a minister, he could come to an Inner Cabinet meeting to make his case, and (2) all ministers are incredibly overworked and being a member of the Inner Cabinet was simply an additional commitment that left less time for other major, and often more interesting, pressing, and rewarding responsibilities.

In addition to the Inner Cabinet, Mr. Clark organized five policy committees — Economic Development, Social and Native Affairs,

Economy in Government, Foreign Policy and Defence, and Federal-Provincial Relations — plus five special committees to deal with legislation and house business, security and intelligence, labour relations, the public service, and routine matters. And, of course, he maintained the one committee created by statute — the Treasury Board.

Mr. Clark also acted to lessen the burden on Cabinet ministers through the appointment of Ministers of State to assist in various activities. Such ministers were appointed for CIDA, Treasury Board, Transport, Fitness and Health, and Multiculturalism, Small Business and Industry, and International Trade. The exact responsibilities of each were worked out, sometimes easily, sometimes with difficulty, with ministers who were being assisted. On occasion the Prime Minister had to intervene to solve marginal problems in assignments, but on balance the system worked well. Originally, it was planned that Ministers of State would not attend Cabinet or committees of Cabinet, but this proved inefficient and unwise and was changed.

When Mr. Trudeau returned to power in 1980, the Cabinet committee system was once again reorganized with special attention directed to relating policy making and resource allocation. And it is certain that as the government evolves and priorities change, that further adjustments will be made. What is not likely to change, however, is the continuous centralization of power. There are no signs of devolution of influence back to the deputies or the departments.

The change in the way in which the central and most powerful decision-making body in Ottawa — the Cabinet — operates has had great consequences on the entire policy-making process in the federal government. It has led to shifts in influence and power from one area of the bureaucracy to another; it has led to a great increase in influence and power of certain positions and a decline in power and influence of others; it has led to the rise of strength of certain advisers and a concomitant loss in influence of others. And very significantly, for anyone who wishes to have an influence in the creation of public policy, it has changed the manner by which the governing and the governed relate to each other. Only through an understanding of these changes is it possible to create strategies for dealing with government and having input into the public policy formulation process.

Power Shifts in Policy Making: The Losers

Ministers and Departments

Obviously, the major losers from the change in the Cabinet decision-making process have been Cabinet ministers who prefer to operate on a highly individualistic basis, arguing their case before Cabinet without sharing responsibility or authority or information with colleagues. Even the most forceful minister, given the manner in which the system for arriving at decisions in Cabinet is now structured, has had to learn to operate within a new framework — a framework that is specifically designed to dilute the power base and influence of any one individual. This does not mean that ministers do not have great power, for indeed they do, or that there are not substantial differences among ministers in their capacity to use power and influence; but it does mean that the system has constrained the power of ministers and lessened the influence of individual departments and this had led to fundamental changes in the way in which policy is formulated. C.D. Howe would not be happy, indeed, could probably not serve in the Cabinet as it functioned in the early 1980s.

Historically, activities of the government of Canada have flowed through departments, and although during the past quarter of a century there has been a bewildering increase in the number of Crown corporations, agencies, commissions, and councils, the department is still the basic unit of government organization. This structure follows from the Cabinet form of government whereby a minister who is responsible to Parliament is appointed to oversee policy formulation, legislation, and operations in a department organized to do the things that the Canadian people have decreed through Parliament they wish to have done.

The nature of departments varies depending on their function. Some are concerned primarily with policy, such as the Department of Finance; others, primarily with the delivery of a service, such as the former Post Office Department. Still others have both policy and service functions, such as the Departments of Agriculture or Industry, Trade and Commerce. Still others co-ordinate policy, such as the Ministry of State for Science and Technology; and others are simply service departments for other departments, such as the Department of Supply and Services. The number of departments and the organization of work within departments vary from time to time depending upon the needs of the nation. During the war, a Department of Munitions and Supply was created; more recently, a Department of Regional Economic Expansion.

It is to the department that citizens look for the carrying out of governmental functions and it is to the department that they often turn when they wish to have an input into policy formulation. In the vast majority of cases, the process of formal policy making begins in the department with the preparation of a memorandum to Cabinet that outlines an issue, the alternative methods for dealing with it, and the proposed action recommended. The memorandum is signed by the minister, and unlike in the earlier period when it went directly to Cabinet where it was discussed by all concerned ministers, it is routed to the appropriate Cabinet committee. When a recommendation is reached by the committee, it is forwarded to Cabinet. Normally the Cabinet will accept the recommendation, but it can be reopened if a minister insists and the Prime Minister agrees. Once a decision is accepted by the Cabinet, the action is recorded in a document known as the Record of Decision, which is used as a basis for instructing departments, or whoever is involved, to proceed to implement the policy.

This apparently straightforward process is, however, incredibly complex. The number of people involved in the preparation of Cabinet documents in any one year is probably well up in the thousands and the number of documents prepared must also approach that number. There is constant discussion of what should be in a memorandum and the amount of conflict and in-fighting that goes on when the issue is of some significance is immense.[9] Because the memorandum is so important, it is not surprising that it has long been the practice of anyone wishing to influence policy to attempt to identify the bureaucrats who may be working on a particular issue so they can inform them, before any proposals become formalized in a memorandum, of the consequences, favourable or unfavourable, of a particular policy initiative.

In spite of the fact that the process for developing and considering various policies does not appear to have changed much over the years, it has. The Cabinet committee system has lessened the impact of the department in the policy-making process. While it is true that a policy may be initiated in a department, there is no certainty that it will go to the Cabinet as proposed because the minister and his officials must now work through the Cabinet committee, and perhaps equally significantly, through the central bureaucracy where their proposals will be reviewed for the chairmen of Cabinet committees, may be delayed, and indeed may be so refined that the essence of an original proposal, if it differs markedly from the general goals of the government, may never reach the Cabinet.

An even more important cause of the decline in power of individual departments has been the formal transfer of the setting of the thrust of the government to the Cabinet Committee on Priorities and Planning, and the growth in the power of the central agencies in advising on policy. The history of the Department of Finance is most instructive on this point, and is of particular significance to the CEO who wishes to influence public policy.

Traditionally, the Department of Finance has been the strongest and most powerful of all government departments. It receives its authority from section 9 of the Financial Administration Act, which gives the Minister of Finance the responsibility for the supervision, control, and direction of all matters relating to the financial affairs of Canada not assigned by law to the Treasury Board or to any other minister. With such authority, it is not astonishing that the department dominated all types of decision making during most of its history. At one time it had over 7,000 employees, but by 1980, because of the continuous change in the operation of government, fewer than 1,000 people were employed in the department.

With the change in the Cabinet decision-making process and the growth in the role of the government in the economy, it is unrealistic to expect that the department could have maintained its jurisdiction over everything associated with economic policy under any circumstances. And yet the department always jealously guarded its prerogatives, and attempts by anyone to move into its jurisdiction were greatly resisted. In the 1960s under the leadership of Robert Bryce, who was Deputy Minister from 1963 to 1970, the battle was fought with some success, primarily because of Bryce's long experience in the public service; but by the 1970s, the department was basically engaged in a rearguard action to maintain its pre-eminence. Instead of embracing the opportunities for leadership that were possible because of its dominant role in Cabinet, and in the Cabinet Economic Policy Committee, of which the minister was chairman, it chose to protect its role as the determinant of stabilization policy through tax and expenditure patterns and it fought desperately to keep any economic expertise out of the other agencies.[10] For example, when Prime Minister Trudeau wished, in the early 1970s, to have a small committee of economists from outside the government meet with him in an informal fashion, the department successfully stopped such an arrangement.

In a sense the department may have won the battle, in fact it could hardly lose, of having the major say in tax and expenditure policy (although even this latter responsibility was seriously challenged in the Clark administration), but it clearly lost the war. As far back as the late 1960s and early 1970s, Gordon Robertson, who was Secretary to the Cabinet and Clerk of the Privy Council at that time, and other senior administrators took the sensible position that policy departments should not be administrative on the grounds that if they were, they would be compromised in their capacity to develop policy in an "objective fashion."[11] For example, when the government decided to reduce regional economic disparities through direct action, it was determined to do so through the creation of a new department — not by adding administrative responsibilities to the Department of Finance.

While there was no deliberate plot to reduce the power and prestige of the department, in fact, during the 1970s the central and all pervasive role of the department in the determination of economic policy declined. When the Clark government came to power in 1979, it found that the critical players in the evaluation and assessment of the economic implications of alternative energy proposals were not the officials in the Department of Finance, but rather the Deputy Minister, Ian Stewart, and the Assistant Deputy Minister, Edmund Clark, both professional economists, of the Department of Energy, Mines and Resources. The officials of the Department of Finance, much to the disappointment of some in the new government, rather than providing ideas and analysis of the economic consequences of the new realities of energy in Canada, basically held a watching brief on the policy process. A decade earlier, it would have been inconceivable for the Department of Finance to have played such a peripheral role in the formulation of any policy with economic implications, no matter how minor, let alone in one as all-encompassing as the policy associated with energy.

The Clark government put great emphasis on the need for new economic policies, and one of its goals was to strengthen the Department of Finance and to re-establish its pre-eminence in the economic decision-making process. It was for this reason that the Minister of Finance, John Crosbie, pressed for — and was given — strong powers. He was able to bring major economic questions to the Inner Cabinet — they were not vetted through the Economic Development Committee — and the management of the two budgetary envelopes Crosbie was responsible for were left with the Inner Cabinet. Finally, he retained the sole responsibility for macro-economic policy although he did have to share with the President of the Treasury Board, which was a major change, the responsibility of setting the total level of expenditures of the government.

The Department of Finance always maintained that total government spending should not necessarily be determined by the amount of money needed to provide the services that the people of Canada wanted at the lowest possible cost, but rather that it must be a function of the amount necessary to provide, in the classic phrase, "full employment with relative price stability."

During the Clark administration, the President of the Treasury Board, Sinclair Stephens, argued for a different approach. He believed that total expenditures of the government should be the cost of provision of appropriately legislated services to the taxpayers. If, after this is determined, additional spending is recommended for some macro-economic goal, that decision should be made on the basis of the situation at the time. To accommodate these two positions it was agreed that the Minister of Finance and the Secretary of the Treasury Board should jointly recommend the total expenditure figure of the government to the Inner Cabinet.

Finally, and most significantly, the Clark government appointed, from outside the public service, a new Deputy Minister of Finance, who was charged with the responsibility of regaining for the department its traditional role as the central power in economic policy making in the government. It was a condition of the appointment of Dr. Reuber — a condition that was not only one of his accepting the position but a condition that was made when the administration offered him the position — that he fulfil this mandate.

Upon the return of the Trudeau government, Ian Stewart was appointed Deputy Minister of Finance. Since Stewart spent several years in the PMO, he will undoubtedly not oppose the further integration of the department into the Cabinet committee system and so the decline in the independent power of the department will contine. Consequently, CEOs who look to the Department of Finance as the department of goverment where the role of the private sector in the economy is most strongly understood and supported should not be sanguine. It is not likely that the department will be as sympathetic a conduit in the future for the views of the private sector to the seats of power in the government as it sometimes has been in the past.

Deputy Ministers

Concomitant with the relative decline in the power of the departments has been a decline in the influence of their chief executive officers — the deputy ministers.

Historically, the deputy ministers of major departments have been among the most influential people in Ottawa. In the 1950s and 1960s, the deputies knew each other well, and they developed such a relationship that among themselves they supplied all the co-ordination among departments that the government needed. They perceived themselves as the permanent element in the government that, regardless of who might be in power, kept the system operating. They had a wide range of acquaintances across the country and prided themselves on the extent of the sources of information they could draw upon in the formulation of policy. And it was the policy function that they cherished most. Indeed, given the way the system operated — the close connection between government and the public service and the formulation of policy — it is not astonishing that many public servants — Mackenzie King, Lester Pearson, Mitchell Sharp, J.W. Pickersgill, to mention the most prominent — found it neither difficult nor inconsistent with the traditional pattern of political neutrality of the public service to move from the role of deputy minister to minister of the Crown. Indeed, it seemed only natural.

The responsibilities of deputy ministers are much broader than simply giving policy advice. They are in fact, although not in law, responsible for the administration of their departments. They must direct, control, staff, and plan, with some limitations, how their departments operate. They co-ordinate and interrelate activities with deputies in other departments, decide what advice to stress, and must work with the central agencies of the government. It is an incredibly difficult and sensitive task, totally time consuming and much more difficult and arduous than is usually recognized by the public.

As the government increased in size after World War II, the work of deputy ministers began to change. The policy function was still important, but the administration of departments became much more significant — and it was not done well. Indeed, general concern about the inadequacy of management in the public service became so great that in the 1950s the government appointed the Royal Commission on Government Operations, chaired by Grant Glassco, to recommend ways in which the management of public funds could be improved. The theme of the Glassco report was to let the "managers manage" by giving the deputy ministers more direct responsibilities for the operations of their departments. Needless to say, with this change in emphasis to administration from policy advising, the priorities of deputies also changed. Knowledge of management and administration became as important for a deputy as knowledge of the substantive issues with which the department dealt.

Since the publication of the final report of the Glassco commission in 1962, governments have sought ways to implement most of its basic recommendations. There has been delegation of responsibility from the Public Service Commission to the departments, and the Treasury Board Secretariat was established as a separate department with the responsibility of establishing standards for the management of personnel and financial resources.[12] In addition, a major effort was mounted within the Treasury Board to evaluate programmes — an effort that failed — but that demonstrated the commitment to try to bring rationality to the expenditures of the resources of government.[13] It was a heady period in the history of the evolution of machinery for the more effective government of the country. It was also a period in which the strength of the individual deputy minister in the overall policy making of the country declined; it helped to hasten the end of the traditional mandarin and the rise in the power and the influence of the technocrat, of the expert in the way the government operated.

In spite of all this, by the mid-1970s it was apparent that the changes brought about as a result of the Glassco commission had not achieved their objectives. Indeed, in 1975, the Auditor General reported that the financial controls of the government of Canada were significantly below acceptable standards and that financial management and control was grossly inadequate.[14] Thus it was clear that the deputy ministers were not properly fulfilling their management responsibilities, and the outcry for reform again became so great that the government had to respond. Consequently it appointed the Royal Commission on Financial Management and Accountability (the Lambert commission), which reported in March of 1979 that "after two years of careful study and consideration, we have reached the deeply held conviction that the serious malaise pervading the management of government stems fundamentally from a grave weakening, and in some cases an almost total breakdown, in the chain of accountability, first within government, and second in the accountability of government to Parliament and ultimately to the Canadian people."[15] It was the contention of this commission that while the Glassco commission achieved some delegation to the managers to manage, such delegation had not been accompanied by implementation of systems that required departments and agencies "to account for the effectiveness of their management to the government itself."[16] To obtain this accountability, the commission recommended a number of measures, among them that deputy ministers should be designated as chief administrative officers of their departments, sign the departments' public accounts, and be responsible to the Public Accounts Committee of the House of Commons for the general administration of their departments. The commission recommended various other changes so that the deputies in fact would have the authority to accept and fulfil the responsibilities given to them.[17]

It also recommended that all deputies be appointed and expected to serve from three to five years in a department. The need for continuity of appointment is obvious. Without some expectation of a reasonable tenure, it is impossible for a senior executive officer to perform his functions and put his stamp on a structure. In addition, in order to ensure that there would be a greater and more consistent emphasis on administrative capacity in top-level positions, the commission recommended that the Secretary for Personnel Management and the Comptroller-General should be advisers on all deputy minister appointments along with the traditional advisers — the Secretary to the Cabinet and the Principal Secretary to the Prime Minister. According to a study done by the commission, many senior officials in Ottawa would applaud such a change.[18]

If the recommendations of the Royal Commission on Financial Management and Accountability are carried out, it will mean more evolution of the role of the deputy minister from that of senior policy adviser to one of manager of resources. Given the requirement for the careful spending of the taxpayers' money, this change may indeed be necessary, but its implications are significant. First, in the selection of deputies, greater emphasis would have to be placed on capabilities and presumably training and experience in traditional management activities: planning, staffing, controlling, directing, and organizing. This would mark a departure from the traditional situation whereby deputies are usually selected because of their understanding of the machinery of government — on their ability to work policies through the system — which means that they are largely chosen from within the system. And second, the significance of the role of deputies in the policy-making process would of necessity have to decline as their responsibilities for administration increased. This would mean even more influence for policy makers at the centre of the system, and this has great implications for the way in which policy is made.

Power Shifts in Policy Making:
The Winners

The development of the full-fledged Cabinet committee system as the central element in policy making created the need for an administrative structure to support the system. Consequently, the Privy Council Office (PCO) and the Prime Minister's Office (PMO) changed dramatically from being centres with mainly staff functions to centres of significant influence in the formulation of government policy. When the power of the departments and the deputies declined, the power of the central agencies and their officers increased.

Until the 1960s, the responsibilities of the PCO were relatively modest. However, with the growth of government the work of the office increased, and by 1970 the PCO was a fully organized secretariat with the functions of recording and following up on actions taken by the Cabinet and keeping the Prime Minister, and Cabinet committee chairmen, informed about the progress of various programmes and activities.

A decade later, in 1980, the responsibilities were even greater and they continue to increase. In fact, the PCO (which can best be understood when thought of as the Prime Minister's department), while not having any direct administrative responsibilities, has great influence in determining the policies of government because it "organizes, co-ordinates and communicates the results of cabinet committee and cabinet meetings . . . [The officials of the PCO] seek to maintain an overview of government policies and programs and, in particular, a continuing sense of the 'cutting edge' of issues and problems which are likely to require collective decision by ministers . . . advise departmental officials about the preparation of Memoranda to Cabinet, establish agendas for cabinet and committee cabinet meetings, brief the Prime Minister and committee chairmen on Memoranda to Cabinet once formally submitted, and draft Committee Reports and Records of Decision."[19]

The exact structure of the PCO constantly changes to meet changing needs. Some idea of the manner in which it operates can be obtained by noting that the function of each secretariat in the late 1970s was as follows:

(1) to monitor developments in the policy sector for which their committee is responsible, including attendance at inter-departmental committee meetings;

(2) to advise departmental officials on the development of Memoranda to Cabinet and Discussion Papers for the signature of ministers;

(3) to draw up, in consultation with the minister who chairs their committee, the Agenda for committee meetings;

(4) to brief the minister who chairs the committee on each item (Memorandum to Cabinet/Discussion Paper) on the Agenda;

(5) to take minutes of committee meetings;

(6) to draw up Committee Reports for each item on the Agenda of the committee;

(7) to provide a briefing for the Prime Minister for every Committee Report on the Cabinet Agenda that originated in their committee;

(8) to disseminate Records of Decision to those departmental and agency officials who should know about them.[20]

In addition, assistant secretaries take minutes of Cabinet meetings and prepare Records of Decision for items decided upon at Cabinet meetings.

Two other very important activities are centred in the PCO: interprovincial relations and staffing.

Because of the increasing volume and complexity of arrangements between the federal government and the provinces, the Federal-Provincial Relations Office (FPRO) was established in 1975 as a distinct organization, but closely linked with the PCO, to assure that all departments followed consistent and interrelated policies in dealing with the provinces. The continuous constitutional turmoil and the growing disagreements about responsibilities of different levels of government assure the FPRO of plenty of activity. It "handles . . . all official communication between the Prime Minister and provincial premiers, selects those issues before Cabinet which the secretariat wishes to review thoroughly, co-ordinates communication from several departments on federal-provincial matters, solicits opinions from provincial governments, briefs the Prime Minister on important issues, and provides a secretariat for federal government delegates to federal-provincial conferences."[21]

Gordon Robertson, who had been Clerk of the Privy Council and Secretary to the Cabinet for more than ten years, was appointed first head of the FRPO and retained his title as Secretary. He held this important responsibility until his retirement from the public service in the winter of 1979.

The total number of contacts between the federal government departments and the provinces is so immense that it is impossible for everything relating to federal-provincial relations to be vetted through the FPRO. At the same time, however, the office is very aware of its prerogatives, and any department with major dealings with a province cannot make major decisions without co-ordinating with the FPRO — another illustration of the centralization of power.

The other important function — and source of power — within the PCO is influence over appointments. The Clerk of the Privy Council serves as Chairman of the Committee of Senior Officials, which reviews the performance of all senior officials on an annual basis and recommends on salary adjustments. The Clerk, along with the Principal Secretary to the Prime Minister, puts before the Prime Minister the list of persons from whom deputy ministers and other top-level appointments are recommended to the Governor in Council. The senior officers in the PCO, therefore, have a decisive impact on the future careers of senior public servants at the top-most level. The real power for senior appointments lies in the PCO — not the Treasury Board — and, indeed, the Clerk of the Privy Council, if he has the full confidence of the Prime Minister who makes the final decision, has great influence in favour of his own choices for key positions at the top of the public service.[22]

The importance of this cannot be over-emphasized. The philosophies, background, and experience of senior officials have a great influence on the nature of the policies that eventually shape the structure of the nation. This was well demonstrated in the Clark administration. For example, senior officials of the Department of Energy, Mines and Resources were uncertain about the wisdom of the privatization of Petro-Canada, and so the government found it extremely difficult to get rapid action on the establishment of the terms of reference for the appointment of a committee to look at the future of that Crown corporation. Or, as another example, it is clear that in the Department of Finance under the deputy-ministership of Simon Reisman, the prevailing philosophy of senior officials was that the private sector and free markets would, within the framework of intelligent monetary and fiscal policies, lead to full employment with relative price stability. Under Tom Shoyama, who worked for many years in the public service of Saskatchewan in a socialist government, it is not astonishing that the non-interventionist philosophy that prevailed with Reisman was less. Grant Reuber, who was appointed deputy minister by Clark, undoubtedly, as his writings indicate, would have been less interventionist than Shoyama, and Ian Stewart, who replaced Reuber, is undoubtedly much more interventionist than Reuber. The point is that the power to influence major appointments is the power to influence the direction of policy, and that power is centred in the PCO.

Given the fact that the senior officials of the PCO prepare the agenda of Cabinet and of Cabinet committees, brief the Prime Minister, influence senior appointments, and oversee federal-provincial relations, it is clear that there can be little significant policy developed by the government that is not monitored and, indeed, greatly influenced by the PCO. Consequently, the views of the Clerk of the Privy Council — the senior public servant in the government — are very influential in determining the thrust of the government.

The Clerk of the Privy Council has always been a professional public servant and, as such, is within the tradition that public servants in Canada do not change when governments change. However, the position of Clerk and Secretary to the Cabinet is unusually sensitive and individual Prime Ministers have made changes during their administrations in order to have a Clerk who fits their style. When Mr. Clark became Prime Minister, he replaced the Clerk, Michael Pitfield, because Pitfield was very closely identified with Mr. Trudeau and his policies. Indeed, Clark had no option. The caucus of the Progressive Conservative Party before the election identified Pitfield as a political partisan, and they would have caused Clark great problems if he had not made a change. When Mr. Trudeau was re-elected, he re-appointed Pitfield as Clerk.

Pitfield is very much a government activist. Indeed, it is his view that "like it or not, over the past couple of decades government has passed decisively from a reactive to an active mode."[23] He perceives it to be the task of the PCO to work constantly to bring about a government with greater efficiency, greater objectiveness, more political (or at least central) control, and more clearly defined objectives. Consequently, he has continued the process, begun in 1968, whereby the PCO has become more involved than it had been previously in the co-ordination of government planning and in preventing individual departments from taking initiatives that are not in conformity with the goals of government as identified, with the help of the PCO, by Cabinet.[24] These trends were muted during the minority Liberal government between 1972 and 1974 but reinforced in the later 1970s.

Obviously the changes in the operations of the PCO caused great changes in the power structure in Ottawa — and they did not occur without considerable conflict. For example, when the staff of the PCO was assigned to work with the Committee on Priorities and Planning "to create . . . a rational *process* and *framework* through which ministers could make decisions,"[25] it was alleged by other members of the bureaucracy to be less than scientific and certainly less than neutral, in spite of the fact that the PCO and its operations were supposed merely to reflect the position of the Cabinet and the ministers.[26]

Although the planning process attempted by the PCO in the 1968–1972 period fell short of its goals, as did a later more broadly based attempt in 1974, the efforts demonstrate — and there are many other examples — that the PCO is much more than a secretariat to the Cabinet. The officials of the PCO are deeply involved in running the machinery of government and are much more than a group of officials recording the will of the Cabinet. The PCO is a centre of great influence with the most important ingredients of influence in Ottawa — access to the Prime Minister and access to information.

The shift in power to the PCO has brought with it a shift in the influence of public servants in Ottawa. The bureaucrats of the PCO are generalists and experts on the way in which the system functions. They are not like the strong deputies of old — experts in a particular area. Rather they are broad conceptual thinkers about the way in which society and the economy should function. They are not readily accessible to the public and they are basically committed to the proposition that the government has the capacity — and the responsibility — to solve a wide variety of problems.

Colin Campbell and George Szablowski surveyed officials in the PCO and PMO in the late 1970s and found that they "tended to describe their roles in terms of improving the structure and operation of government, facilitating actual decisions, and performing independent analyses of departments' proposals. . . . [They] represent practically every academic discipline, although lawyers are clearly more numerous . . . [and] . . . despite the conventional wisdom that officials circulate through the PCO and FPRO rapidly, . . . the average tenure is fairly long. . . . Despite their current involvement in the policy process, [they] minimize policy roles in their statements of career objectives. . . . [They] interact quite readily with the PM, Ministers, and top officials of other departments. They frequently participate on interdepartmental and cabinet panels concerned with broad issues . . . [and they] . . . clearly keep outsiders at a distance. Generally, they do not believe that they are even partly accountable to the public and they rarely consult outsiders. . . . this lack of a sense of public accountability . . . suggests that they live in a detached world indeed. . . ."[27]

The majority of officials in the PCO "stressed management as an area of their expertise"[28] and "the largest proportion of officials . . . acquired their expertise from experiences in government. . . . It appears . . . that [they] . . . learn on the job. Private-sector experiences are not thought crucial to their present work, while public-service experience is granted considerable importance. . . ."[29]

Although they consider themselves as administrators or managers, the fact is that the staff of the PCO has little professional experience or training in management. As a consequence, it is not surprising that they are sceptical of the possibility of adapting management techniques from the private sector to the administration of government.

Because of their influence over appointments, the Secretaries to the Cabinet have been able to argue successfully for putting in most departments deputy ministers who share the view that the principal qualification for a senior public servant is to be able to operate within the system — to be a generalist rather than a specialist. As a result, the inclination, to say nothing of the power, of individual departments to take independent action on a specific issue has been eroded. There are no longer any departments or deputy ministers with anything like the capacity or, indeed, the desire to challenge the system or the policies that the central system produces. The end result of this for anyone who wishes to have significant influence on broad policy issues is that he must find a method of dealing with the central agencies, something that is not always easy to do.

Deputy ministers, of course, still advise — and advise with great influence — on policy in their own areas. They are still the most important single source of advice to a minister. Consequently, CEOs with particular problems or proposals that fall within the purview of any one department would be ill-advised to ignore the deputy in any search for a solution to a difficulty or any attempt to have a proposal adopted. However, they should not expect that the deputies are the vehicle through which the private sector can alter the general thrust or direction of general government policy, they simply no longer have that type of influence.

The Prime Minister's Office

The function of the Prime Minister's Office (PMO) is "to serve the Prime Minister in the exercise of his powers, in the pursuit of his duties, in the discharge of his responsibilities,"[30] and as those duties and responsibilities change, the nature of the office changes. Basically, these services include, as well as others, the following:

1. provision for the personal needs of the Prime Minister, such as his travel arrangements and hospitality to official visitors;
2. management of the Prime Minister's schedule and of access to him;
3. briefing of the Prime Minister for his participation in Question Period in the House of Commons;
4. management of the Prime Minister's voluminous correspondence;
5. linkage of the Prime Minister with the party apparatus in Ottawa and across the country;
6. communications and media relations;
7. political advice regarding potential appointees to part-time positions in the Governor in Council group;
8. political advice on major issues of policy and priorities and on parliamentary and electoral strategy.[31]

The PMO is headed by a Principal Secretary or Chief of Staff and the operation of the department, other than for routine matters, is determined to a considerable degree by the nature of the Secretary and his relationship to the Prime Minister. It is generally recognized that Marc Lalonde played an exceptionally important role in helping Prime Minister Trudeau assess the performance of the government, the activity of various members of the public service, and the effectiveness of various policy thrusts. He spent a great deal of time working with the PCO to settle disagreements between various departments and ministers. Lalonde had great influence and power when he was Principal Secretary.

Other Secretaries have been different. Martin O'Connell, during his term of office, was clearly less powerful, primarily because he was not regarded as close to the Prime Minister. He concentrated on the administration of the Office — of seeing that the Prime Minister's administrative needs were met. Jack Austin, who was rewarded for his work as Principal Secretary by an appointment to the Senate, tried to re-introduce the Lalonde style and succeeded to a considerable degree, although his attempts to introduce a system for more effective priority setting and planning are generally recognized as failures. Jim Coutts was primarily an administrator and political strategist who constantly appraised the Prime Minister's activities in the context of their political implications.

Under the Clark administration, the office was held by Bill Neville, who was much in the Lalonde mould. Neville was the person through whom Clark tried to get things done. He constantly interrelated with ministers, wrote speeches, gave political advice, and was a strong and powerful force — perhaps the single strongest force in the Clark administration. Before joining Clark, he had extensive experience in government, in business, and in the electoral process, which enabled him to establish contact and rapport with a large number of private-sector people — and he maintained that rapport and the contacts while Principal Secretary to the Prime Minister. He was accessible and provided a ready way for various concerned businessmen to advance their views to the Prime Minister. Neville had, as did Lalonde, considerable influence on the policy-making process during the Clark administration.

The input of the PMO into policy making has differed greatly over the past decade, depending on the relationship of the Prime Minister to the PCO and to his Principal Secretary. Clearly, under Trudeau, who has a particularly close relationship with Michael Pitfield, the PCO dominates the policy-making function. However, the PMO has an input in assessing the political implications of a particular policy, and occasionally plays a greater role when the Prime Minister has a special interest in a particular area or wishes to have advice independent to that which he may receive from a department. For example, from 1970 to 1978, Ivan Head was in the PMO as senior adviser for international relations, primarily because Trudeau was interested in external affairs and wanted close association with them. Another policy post — Assistant Principal Secretary for Plans and Policy — filled by Michael Kirby of Dalhousie University — was established when the Prime Minister and Pitfield wanted to develop priorities for the government and to monitor how the government was succeeding in developing programmes in harmony with the priorities.

After Kirby left, his replacement, Brian Fleming, defined his responsibility as basically dealing with short-term problems. Major policy input was no longer as significant a function in the PMO.

When Prime Minister Clark was elected, he perceived his policy needs from the PMO to be somewhat different than had Mr. Trudeau. Not astonishingly, given the fact that he had a new Clerk of the Privy Council, an inexperienced ministry, and no clear knowledge of how the public service would react to his election — and to his changing the Clerk of the Privy Council — Mr. Clark wanted a capacity for major input in policy in the PMO. He was determined to get on well with the public service,[32] but he also wanted policy inputs from sources other than the public sector. As a consequence, he appointed me as senior policy adviser reporting directly to him.

Mr. Clark and I had gotten to know each other during the period 1972–1978 when we were both Members of Parliament. After he became Leader of the Progressive Conservative Party, he asked me to serve as Chairman of the Committee of Chairmen, more commonly called the Shadow Cabinet, and in that capacity we worked closely together in the evolution of policy and the evaluation of the capacity of various members of the caucus to initiate policy. Unlike Mr. Stanfield, who wanted a very loose opposition organization, Mr. Clark wanted a tight structure.

Although I had decided in 1978 not to seek re-election, when the election was called in 1979 Clark asked me to advise him during the national campaign. After the election, I participated actively in discussions about structure of Cabinet, major policy thrusts, and the organization of the government. At that point I agreed to stay on as senior policy adviser until 1 January 1980.

Because of the nature of my background and my close relationships as a colleague in Parliament with the members of the new Cabinet, Mr. Clark asked me to participate in many of the early policy decisions, particularly in the fields of economics and energy. Indeed, for the first few months of the new administration, we met both formally and informally on these and all types of related issues on a daily basis. By any definition, during the early days of the Clark government, there was major policy input from the PMO on most issues, and the conventional wisdom in Ottawa was that the policy-making function so strongly ensconced in the PCO during the last months of the Trudeau government was moving to the PMO.

My mode of operation and my short-term commitments to the position did not lend themselves to the construction of a regular policy division. Neville, however, wanted to emulate the Kirby model (1974–1976) to the extent of having briefing notes for the Prime Minister on the political implications of various actions accompanying the briefing notes of the PCO on the administrative implications of actions. Consequently, two political analysts were hired, assigned to monitor various Cabinet secretariats and the beginning of a policy organization was created. The structure was at the time very loose, but if the government had not fallen, it is certain that a policy group of some significance would have been developed in the PMO.

Some political experts believe that this type of development is proper and important. They "believe that the Prime Minister is entitled to a first-class policy-advisory staff independent from the cabinet secretariat ... [because the] PCO and FPRO officials are too career oriented and technocratic to provide policy advice that gives adequate consideration both to the political aspects of problems and to public accountability."[33] I do not agree.

The fact is that in the Cabinet system of government, policy theoretically should come from the departments through the ministers. Under the Trudeau system, whereby the Cabinet committees and the PCO play such a large role, it does not always work this way, but the initiation of policy is usually a departmental responsibility. A very senior person close to the Prime Minister who is perceived, or is actually able, to countermand a minister, is in an unenviable position and in time may become a problem rather than an asset. The fact of the matter is that on any issue that must be settled within a reasonable time-frame, the Prime Minister cannot be put in the position of not supporting his minister, unless he wants a very serious situation on his hands. And yet, this can well happen if a senior policy adviser takes issue with the type of advice being given by the department. The flagging of political problems is important and the evolution of a system to do so is also important, but most political difficulties do not manifest themselves in broad policy formulation but rather in implementation and explanation.

In the last analysis, a senior policy adviser in the PMO is basically a fire-fighter and from time to time a supporter of various ministers. For example, it was clear shortly after the Clark administration was sworn in that there was not whole-hearted enthusiasm in the Department of Finance for the government's policy that homeowners' interest payments on residential mortgages, up to a specified amount, should be deductible in the calculation of personal income taxes. It was useful to the Prime Minister to have someone in his office who could, with the authority of the Prime Minister, lend support to the Minister of Finance in getting the department to move on the proposal in time for its inclusion in the budget. It was also important for the Prime Minister to have someone in his office who could accompany officials as they visited their counterparts in the provinces in an attempt to develop an energy policy and, indeed, to have someone who knew the principal political players in the operation. It is important to have a monitoring structure to see that no significant political issue is overlooked in the evolution of policy and, of course, the Prime Minister must have people whom he trusts with whom he may discuss issues of policy privately, but the less formal the structure in the Canadian situation, the more effective it will be.

The rather *ad hoc* nature of the PMO underlines how important it is for anyone interested in policy formulation to assess and follow the way in which any Prime Minister uses the office. Because of their responsibilities, the senior staff of the PMO are usually accessible to the public and at the senior level they are very influential. They should not be ignored by anyone attempting to have an input into the formulation of policy.

The Executive Decision-Making Process: How Will It Change in the 1980s?

While the Diefenbaker and Pearson administrations were often, and probably correctly, described as administratively inefficient and inadequate for their time, the fact is that public administration in Canada up until the end of the Pearson era had certain clearly identifiable features. It was characterized by the prominence and power of very strong ministers and very strong deputy ministers and departments. The consequence of this for anyone dealing with the government was clear: one knew with whom to deal, one knew where the power to make decisions rested, and one knew who had influence. In the 1970s — the Trudeau years — this situation changed and because it was changed, the relationship between government and business also changed. The old-boy's network began to erode in the late 1960s and had virtually disappeared by the 1970s. With its demise went the intimate relationship — the élite accommodation — which had characterized so much of Ottawa's decision making in the post–World War II period. By 1980, there was a new type of deputy minister in charge — one who had probably served in his department only a short period of time, who was an expert in the way the government operated, and who saw his task as much one of accommodating his department to the central thrust of the government as it was of putting forward his department's or his department's clients' views. Advice to the government on the appropriateness of policies came more from the central advisers than from strong deputy ministers working among themselves.

The system put in place in the 1970s was designed to bring greater efficiency, greater effectiveness, more political control, and the capability of clearly defining the objectives of government. "[It] was almost a total rejection of the personalized [approach] in the 1950s and early 1960s. . . . [It meant that] the management of government became institutionalized and formal."[34] And yet, by the beginning of the 1980s, there was no clear-cut evidence that the system was accomplishing what it had been designed to do.

Four major objections have been raised about it. First, it is a slow and cumbersome process requiring incredible inputs which, of course, are not costless. Second, it has led to the creation of a large central bureaucracy somewhat unidentifiable and clearly not accountable to Parliament in the normal manner. Third, it has caused a redistribution of power in the bureaucracy from the line departments to the centre and this has created a new type of bureaucratic power — the power of the generalist — of the person who knows how the system works as opposed to the person who is an expert in a substantive area of knowledge; and fourth, it has strengthened the power of the Prime Minister *vis-à-vis* other ministers because (1) it forces ministers to feed their ideas and concepts through a central system that the Prime Minister controls, and (2) it lessens the power of any individual department's bureaucracy.

It has been argued that the consequence of this system is that particularly strong ministers — strong in the sense of assurance about what should be done in their particular area — will not stay in a system where there are so many opportunities for their ideas to be blocked, changed, or delayed. It is also alleged that the system has not, as it was intended, noticeably increased the power of the elected representatives of the people in the decision-making process by lessening the power of the senior public servants, but rather has changed the public servants who have power.

In addition, there is considerable evidence that the system has not been effective in achieving some of its own self-imposed goals. For example, studies now available on the efficiency of the system in dealing with planning and priorities, or in evolving an industrial structure, record a decade with more failures than successes.[35]

Moreover, there are indications that in the making of very major decisions — decisions that are fundamental to the direction of the nation — the system has not worked at all. For example, the policy-making process has not been able to bring constraint into government spending — a key priority of all governments over the past few years. The inability of the system to cope with the spending problem is indicated by the fact that when Prime Minister Trudeau returned from the Bonn Summit in 1978 determined to cut back on government expenditures, he announced on television that expenditures would be reduced by $2.5 billion, and then informed his ministers and the bureaucracy to make such cuts. He had given up on the capacity of the system to achieve the policy goal of reducing expenditures.

Similarly, the energy policy of Prime Minister Clark, which was based on the need to move Canada from a position of self-reliance on oil to self-sufficiency, was not developed through the system. It was based primarily on "top-down" policy-making processes. While it may be argued that neither of these initiatives outside of "the system" worked — expenditures continued to increase albeit at a reduced rate — and although he had worked out an agreement in principle with the producing provinces with respect to energy, the Clark government fell primarily because of energy policy — there is no question that policy developed in these two areas did not come through the formal policy process so painstakingly put in place during the 1970s.

In the 1980s, as in the 1950s, and as will probably always be true, the top-down system of decision making was still being used in Canada in major policy areas. And this is a very important point for CEOs to remember. The fact that a new decision-making process has been put in place does not mean that decisions are not made by specific individuals holding important positions in government. But in the 1980s, they are different people in different positions than in the 1950s. Moreover, they are people who do not necessarily relate to the private sector and who may have a very different view of the appropriate role of government, and therefore of the private sector, in society than do businessmen. And they certainly have different perceptions about the way government should operate than did the mandarins and ministers of the 1950s.

The search for new and improved ways of making policy in government is a continuing process. The two most important developments at the beginning of the 1980s were the introduction of a new budgetary process, which attempts to relate decisions for the inauguration of programmes to the amount of money available to support them — called the envelope system,[36] and the establishment of ministries for economic development and social development supported by their own secretariats. The hope is that the ministries will be able to co-ordinate development and administration of policies in these broad areas of government activity.

And changes will continue to be made. What the direction of such changes will be is not, however, clear. With the need for control over expenditures and accountability, plus greater recognition of the fact that in spite of any system that may be put in place, at some point there must be authority and responsibility exercised by individuals, there may well be more application of private-sector management methods into government. The rise of the multinational firm operating in a variety of environments, producing a multiplicity of products, employing thousands of workers, and responding to pressures that management never before experienced has led to the evolution of new techniques and practices of administration, many of which have never been used in government. Clearly, there are major differences between the management of the public and the private sectors, but perhaps instead of building on the differences, which has been the tendency in the past decade, there will be efforts to build on the similarities. One cannot dispute the contention that the "methods of modern management have become the wonder of contemporary social organization,"[37] and that one of the pressing challenges of government administrators is to determine how these methods can be adapted to assist the process of policy making in the public sector.

Whether attempts to improve government policy making in the 1980s will move in this direction will depend, to a very great extent, not on institutions and organizations, but on the philosophy and leadership of the people searching for ways and means of making government decision making more effective. The need for private-sector managers to play a role in the search — of taking an active part in improving the process of government — has never been greater or more challenging: yet another reason why the CEO should become involved in the public sector.

The changing way in which policy is formulated in Ottawa has had a dramatic impact on the way in which the private sector, indeed all elements in society, interface with government. While the collective power of the Cabinet is probably as great as it has ever been, the power of ministers as individuals to decide and to control within their specific jurisdictions has clearly declined. Consequently, the traditional approach of the CEO meeting with the minister is clearly less effective than it was two decades ago: ministers, as individuals, simply do not have the power that they once possessed.

Similarly, the influence of the deputy minister is much less. Because the indepenent power of strong ministers has declined, so has the influence of the deputy, and as this has happened the impact of the central agency officers has increased. To the extent that the deputy of a department can and does work closely with the public servants in the central agencies, his influence is significant. But it is worth noting that in terms of establishing the major policy directions of the government, in most cases, much more influence is now wielded by the senior central agency advisers and much less by those in the departments than was the case in the past.

This is not to argue that it is unimportant for CEOs and other officers of corporations to meet with and attempt to influence various department officials. On certain specific issues it is essential that they do so. Nor is it to suggest that power is no longer with the Cabinet minister for, of course, it is. But it is important to note that power over specific areas is more limited — it is more shared than was the case two decades ago. Moreover, the former overwhelming power of certain departments, particularly that of the Department of Finance, has decreased substantially.

The implications of these changes for anyone wishing to influence policy making in the nation are very large, and to the extent that the changes are not recognized and acted upon, the potential for influencing policy is diminished. Certainly the CEO who believes that a trip to see the minister or the deputy will solve his problem is operating on a false premise. The age of "élite accommodation" in business-government relations in Canada is largely over.

Notes

[1] Andrew Roman, "Comment" on W.T. Stanbury, "Lobbying and Interest Group Representation in the Legislative Process," in *The Legislative Process in Canada: The Need for Reform*, edited by W.A.W. Neilson and J.C. MacPherson (Montreal: The Institute for Research on Public Policy, 1978), p. 215.

[2] Milton Friedman, *Essays in Positive Economics* (Chicago: University of Chicago Press, 1953), p. 4.

[3] See Appendix C.

[4] Robert Bothwell and William Kilbourn, *C.D. Howe: A Biography* (Toronto: McClelland and Stewart, 1979), p. 262.

[5] In spite of the fact that Mr. Diefenbaker had publicly acknowledged the good work of his Clerk of the Privy Council, Robert Bryce, it has become folklore within the Progressive Conservative Party that Mr. Diefenbaker's government was sabotaged by the public service.

[6] Gordon Robertson, "The Changing Role of the Privy Council Office," *Canadian Public Administration* 14 (Winter 1971), p. 490.

[7] *Ibid.*, p. 491.

[8] "When Pierre Elliott Trudeau won the leadership of the Liberal party in 1968, two crucial elements coalesced in an extraordinary way. First, at the institutional level, the existing structure of government became visibly inadequate to meet the rapidly multiplying demands made on government by various segments of Canadian society, so that things were ripe in Ottawa for a major change. Second, the philosophical approach of the new leader, which combined an intense commitment to rationality with the pursuit of functional, pragmatic politics, suited the needs of the moment." Colin Campbell and George J. Szablowski, *The Superbureaucrats: Structure and Behaviour in Central Agencies* (Toronto: Macmillan, 1979), p. 8.

[9] Douglas Hartle, *The Draft Memorandum to Cabinet* (Toronto: Institute of Public Administration of Canada, 1976).

[10] Richard D. French, *How Ottawa Decides: Planning and Industrial Policy-Making 1968–1980.* (Toronto: Canadian Institute for Economic Policy, 1980), p. 30.

[11] Personal correspondence with Gordon Robertson.

[12] Royal Commission on Financial Management and Accountability, *Final Report* (Ottawa: Minister of Supply and Services Canada, 1979), pp. 23–24.

[13] Douglas G. Hartle, *Public Policy Decision Making and Regulation* (Montreal: The Institute for Research on Public Policy, 1979), pp. 173–96.

[14] *Report of the Auditor General of Canada to the House of Commons for the Fiscal Year Ended March 31, 1976* (Ottawa: Minister of Supply and Services Canada, 1976), p. 9.

[15] Royal Commission on Financial Management and Accountability, *Final Report, op. cit.*, p. 21.

[16] Royal Commission on Financial Management and Accountability, *Summary of the Final Report* (Ottawa: Royal Commission on Financial Management and Accountability, 1979), p. 6.

[17] Royal Commission on Financial Management and Accountability, *Final Report, op. cit.*, Chapter 7.

[18] *Ibid.*, p. 197.

[19] French, *op. cit.*, p. 6.

[20] Richard D. French, "The Privy Council Office: Support for Decision Making," in *The Canadian Political Process*, 3d ed., edited by Richard Schultz, Orest M. Kruhlak, and John C. Terry (Toronto: Holt, Rinehart & Winston, 1979), p. 374.

[21] Campbell and Szablowski, *op. cit.*, p. 85.

[22] The Committee on Senior Officials also advises the Prime Minister on bilingualism policy, conflict-of-interest problems, difficulties between ministers and senior public servants, post-employment regulations, and the work of special groups from time to time such as the Royal Commission on Financial Management and Accountability.

[23] Michael Pitfield, "The Shape of Government in the 1980s: Techniques and Instruments for Policy Formulation at the Federal Level," *Canadian Public Administration* 19 (Spring 1976), p. 9.

[24] *Ibid.*, p. 15.

[25] French, *How Ottawa Decides, op. cit.*, p. 43. Emphasis in original.

[26] *Ibid.*

[27] Campbell and Szablowski, *op. cit.*, pp. 220–21. They also studied the Treasury Board and the Department of Finance in depth.

[28] *Ibid.*, p. 142.

[29] *Ibid.*, p. 143.

[30] Marc Lalonde, "The Changing Role of the Prime Minister's Office," *Canadian Public Administration* 14 (Winter 1971), p. 518.

[31] French, "The Privy Council Office: Support for Cabinet Decision Making," *op. cit.*, p. 385.

[32] It is a well-held view in the Progressive Conservative Party that Mr. Diefenbaker was not served well by the public service. The Honourable Alvin Hamilton maintains that this is a fact; the Honourable George Hees maintains that it is not. Regardless, shortly after being sworn in, Clark arranged to meet all deputy ministers to explain his philosophy of government. By all reports it was an extremely encouraging start for the new government.

[33] Campbell and Szablowski, *op. cit.*, pp. 230–31.

[34] M. Kirby and H.V. Kroeker, "The Politics of Crisis Management in Government: Does Planning Make a Difference?" in *Studies on Crisis Management*, edited by C.F. Smart and W.T. Stanbury (Montreal: The Institute for Research on Public Policy, 1978), p. 185.

[35] See French, *How Ottawa Decides*, *op. cit.*

[36] Treasury Board, *Guide to the Policy and Expenditure Management System* (Ottawa: Minister of Supply and Services Canada, 1980).

[37] Derek Bok, *The President's Report 1977–1978* (Cambridge: Harvard University, 1977), p. 10.

Parliament, Politics, and the CEO

7

In the Canadian legislative system, bills that reflect the policy of the government are presented to Parliament by the executive and become law only after they are enacted by the legislature — the House of Commons and the Senate.[1] The members of the Senate are appointed but the members of the House of Commons are elected, usually as members of a political party, and the party with the most members forms the government. It is logical to assume therefore that Parliament and political parties are very powerful, since presumably if Parliament disagrees with something it can never become law, no matter how much the executive may want it.

However, most CEOs and almost all analysts of the governmental process know that the power of the legislature is extremely limited. It is widely believed in Ottawa that if an idea is drafted into the form of legislation, it is almost certain to be enacted. It is not the legislature, but the executive and the public service that have the power — at least they have much more impact on the formulation of public policy than Members of Parliament, either individually or collectively. Prime Minister Trudeau's comment that twenty miles from Parliament Hill M.P.'s are "nobodies" is well known.

In spite of all these negative reports about the power of Parliament, when members of the private sector decry the nature of government policy, they are told that if they do not like it they should get actively involved in politics, that they should run for political office. Indeed, in 1978 a poll conducted by the Institute for Political Involvement resulted in a majority of those interviewed stating that if the private sector was to have an appropriate influence on public policy, more businessmen should run for election to the House of Commons.[2]

W.M. Lee, a professional observer of the government scene, has commented that "business people have got to stop copping out of the most important way in which to influence the thrust of government policy — the actual running for public office — if we are to have some balance in the creation of public policy."[3]

But does it matter? If, as one disillusioned businessman who entered the process and served in the House of Commons believes, that "in

Canadian politics, the prime minister ... has become the chief executive officer. He is the president and not just the chairman of the board ... the real influence on decision-making rests with a small group of advisers who may or may not be members of Cabinet"[4] is correct, why get involved in politics?

The reasons are obvious. First, in the Canadian system, it is through the political process that the executive branch of government — the Prime Minister and the Cabinet — is chosen, and no one doubts the influence and power of these offices, particularly that of Prime Minister. If one is not in politics, one can never attain the apex of power.[5] Second, political parties do have influence and elected Members of Parliament do influence the position taken by parties. And third, the legislative side of government is in critical need of reform, and that reform will not come about through the efforts of the professional politicians — those who make a career out of politics — but only from non-career-oriented people who see the staggering necessity of making the legislative side of the parliamentary system work. Businessmen who have experience and background in manage- ment and decision making can be extremely important in bringing reform. The system cannot be rejected; it is all there is and it is probably the best form of government ever invented by man. The fact that it is not working well is not a reason to stay out of the political process, but rather a compelling one for becoming involved.

A well-functioning legislature is extremely important in a pluralis- tic society because it is in Parliament where all interests in the policy-making process ought to be reconciled. And it is to the legislature that all sectors of society must look for countervailing influence to the executive branch of government. For the private sector, the absence of a powerful legislature is particularly critical given the proclivity for the executive to increase the role of govern- ment in the economy. Reform of the parliamentary system has to be a prime objective of any strategy on the part of business to assure input in the determination of the public interest.

Parliament and the Formulation of Policy

Parliament, it is said, has three basic functions that may be described as financial, legislative, and critical. Of these, most observers would say only the critical is being performed at anything close to acceptable levels. The other two are not, by any standard, done well, Indeed, in spite of the fact that the House of Commons usually meets eleven months a year, with both day and evening sittings, every session ends without action on important legislation. There are always program- mes mentioned in the Speech from the Throne that do not get enacted, even though they are high-priority items for the government.

It is, however, in the basic function of overseeing the expenditure of the taxpayers' money that parliamentary activity has almost completely broken down, and yet parliamentary control of spending is a basic principle of parliamentary government. The essence of responsible government and "the key to Parliament's role as a body to which accountability is owed for the administration of government has always been the need for Parliament's approval of government expenditure and its power to review that expenditure."[6] In Canada, it is a fiction to believe that Parliament exercises such power. The fact is that "the Government's ability to build and defend strong policy positions has been greatly enhanced by the growth of the public service ... the Crown is assisted in what is now only a sporadic struggle with Parliament by the research and policy-making expertise of thousands of civil servants" to the point where "the relationship is so unequal that the principles of responsible government, while still generally accepted, are in danger of becoming irrelevant to the actual situation."[7] The most exhaustive study of the capacity of Parliament to fulfil one of the most fundamental of all its functions, namely reviewing the spending of the people's money, concludes that there is no effective review or control of expenditures, that in the early 1980s proper financial management of the taxpayers' money simply did not exist.

Parliament operates with a rather extensive committee system, a practice that in parliamentary terms is relatively new. Indeed, before World War II, committees were practically unheard of. In that simpler time when the government was not so involved in so many things, Parliament was able to process legislation and consider expenditures sitting as a Committee of the Whole — that is, in the House of Commons itself. After the war, with an increase in government activity, committees were occasionally struck, but they were used in an irregular, haphazard, and intermittent manner. Indeed, Prime Ministers King and St. Laurent thought of committees as much like Royal Commissions, "suitable repositories for issues which were politically volatile or on which the Government was divided or had no firm policies."[8]

Mr. Diefenbaker, on the other hand, had throughout his career as a private member argued for the right of Members of Parliament to have more effective forums within which to examine legislation and expenditures. Consequently, when he became Prime Minister, he supported the use of committees and under his administration the Public Accounts Committee was established with the provisions that (1) the chairman be a member of the opposition, (2) it meet each year, and (3) it receive the reports of the Auditor General — a major step forward in the development of the House of Commons committee system.

Mr. Pearson did not have a strong interest in the use of committees, possibly because of his background in the public service, but with the increasing work of Parliament it was apparent by the beginning of the 1960s that if Parliament was to function, major changes had to be made. After considerable study the Procedure Committee of the House in its Fifteenth Report, released on 15 December 1964, recommended the establishment of a complete committee system, and in the First Session of the Twenty-Eighth Parliament in 1968 and 1969, major far-reaching reforms were enacted.

The essence of the reforms was to do away with the *ad hoc* nature of the committee system. Standing committees were created, nine of which were basically concerned with estimates and legislation corresponding to government activities. The expenditure estimates were referred automatically to an appropriate committee, which in turn was required to report its findings back to the House of Commons on a specified date. All legislation was sent to a committee for examination, unless the House itself specifically ruled otherwise. In addition, it was agreed that special committees would seldom be appointed, that membership on committees would be as continuous as possible, and that appointment would be for the duration of Parliament, not a single session.

While the integration of the committee system into the structure of Parliament was an essential reform — no government could deal with the myriad problems on its agenda without such a change — committees in the early 1980s were still basically ineffective. The chairmen of all but the Public Accounts Committee are appointed by the executive, and membership on committees is proportionate to membership in the House of Commons, and so a government with a majority in the House always has a majority of committee members. Indeed, the executive sees committees, by and large, not primarily as instruments for changing or improving legislation or the challenging of spending, but rather as vehicles for getting their legislative programmes enacted. In no significant way are committees independent of the executive, and therefore it is not astonishing that they do not act as a check on executive activities.

Even if they were not tied so closely to the executive, the manner in which committees are managed would make them ineffective. Committees have little or no staff, and members do not have the competence to investigate seriously most matters referred to them. On occasion, on very specific topics, a particular member may be able to elicit information, but not often. Questioning is rotated among members with each questioner given only ten minutes at a time, so it is seldom that any systematic series of questioning takes place. Committee hearings are normally not televised, as is the House of Commons, and their activities are not reported by the media. Since for many M.P.'s electoral survival depends on publicity, committee work has no particular attraction.

Even the way in which the committee is physically structured works against the committee member. The witness, usually a minister accompanied by a number of officials, sits at the head of the table and the questioning committee members are ranged below the witness on either side. There is no legal advice for a committee member and, of course, no experienced professional advisers comparable to the public officials accompanying a minister. In short, the system is one of form, not substance, and in terms of examining estimates, that is, expenditure of the government, it is ineffective.

With respect to legislation, committees can occasionally be more useful. Amendments can and are introduced and quite often committee hearings are the occasions for the government itself to make corrections to legislation. Indeed, if there is a particularly poorly drafted bill, the committee hearings provide a final opportunity for corrections to be made. In addition, a committee may hear witnesses with respect to legislation and, as a result, changes in detail, although not in substance, may occur.[9] However, no one should be under any illusion that changes that the government is not aware of or that it does not want will be accepted by a committee.

On particularly significant issues the government may refer a White Paper — a statement of general policy possibilities — to a committee so that it may hold hearings on the issue. However, again no changes are proposed that are not generally acceptable to the government. For example, during the examination of the *White Paper on Taxation* in the late 1960s, the committee "heard 211 briefs and 820 individuals (it received a total of 524 briefs and 1,093 letters and other submissions), held 146 meetings, and digested this bookshelf full of information into a hundred page report. . . . but the extent to which its recommendations [were] adopted [reflected] prior understanding between Liberal committee members, and government, as there were many informal discussions between them and Mr. Benson, the Minister of Finance, during the investigation."[10]

The committee system of the Parliament of Canada is totally unlike that of the United States Congress, and their functions should not be confused. In the United States, as is well known, the executive and the legislative functions are totally independent, and the arms of government interact totally differently than they do in Canada. Moreover, committees of the United States House of Representatives and Senate have large professional staffs, as do individual congressmen and senators, and so hearings are professionally staffed and run. Such is far from the case in Canada, and so there is no serious scrutiny of expenditures or legislation. In short, committees that have significant responsibilities do not have the power or structure to fulfil their obligations.

Not all assessments of the work of the committees of the House of Commons are negative. The Honourable John Reid, a Member of Parliament for many years, argues that the committee system provides the back-bencher with "both his best opportunity and his greatest frustrations . . . [and] his greatest opportunity to influence the actual words of the law."[11] In addition, special committees are sometimes appointed to examine various problems thoroughly and to make recommendations for legislation, and occasionally they can have some influence although the presentation of recommendations far from guarantees legislation. In addition, the Auditor General reports to the Standing Committee on Public Accounts, and quite often as a result of his work, the committee is put on the track of major problems and can bring about reform, as was the case, for example, with the Atomic Energy Commission of Canada.

However, in spite of the defence that is put forward, the committees are not effective, both in absolute terms and relative to the time and money spent on them. While some have suggested that the ineffectiveness of committees is a result of the turnover in the membership of the House of Commons and therefore the inexperience of many committee members, an alternative, and perhaps more likely, hypothesis may well be that the ineffectiveness of committees is a major reason why many talented and committed people feel that they can better utilize their time and efforts in the public interest somewhere other than in the House of Commons. The fact is that "the private member has been reduced to little more than a rubber stamp"[12] and the "system under-utilizes . . . the talents and efforts of . . . conscientious members."[13] In the words of one thoughtful member, all there is "today is a minuet of committees . . . [where] . . . government members fall neatly into file and toe the party line."[14]

Chief executive officers, in spite of the fact that the committee system provides them a forum for commenting on legislation, have something less than admiration for the way in which committees function. Indeed, one CEO has stated that "one of the most frustrating experiences in my professional life was appearing before a Parliamentary Committee," while another pointed out that when "draft legislation gets to the committee stage our parliamentary machinery does not provide for the kind of effective analysis which takes place in the United States Congress."[15]

Given the fact that Parliament, in its important functions, is not operating as it should, it is not surprising that a number of proposals have been advanced for parliamentary reform. Most recommendations relate to fixed dates for opening and closing, fixed dates for election (unless the government is defeated in the House), and so on, but the most significant proposals call for major reform and overhaul in the operation of the committees.

Chief executive officers of Canadian corporations are well aware of the need for change. Indeed, the first study commissioned by the Business Council on National Issues, the major collective voice of Canadian senior executives, was on parliamentary reform. The report,[16] which was widely commended, although apparently not extremely influential in bringing change, recommends among other things that:

(i) The government refer possible policy initiatives to committees early in the policy formulation process so that individual members of parliament and the public can make inputs into the formulation of possible policy long before there is any commitment to legislation.

(ii) The size of committees be reduced from 20 to 14 with a corresponding reduction in the size of the quorum.

(iii) Substitution of membership on committees be limited.

(iv) The chairman be elected by a majority vote of the members of the committee.

(v) The chairman be paid a stipend similar to that paid to a parliamentary secretary.

(vi) Committees be given staff.

(vii) Provision be made for televising certain committee hearings.

(viii) The House of Commons work program be cycled on a five-week basis so that the House meets for three weeks, committees one, with one week closed so that members may attend to constituency business.

(ix) A major on-going review of changes in tax policy be made by the Standing Committee on Finance, Trade and Economic Affairs, and that the technical and structural tax aspects of a bill be separated from the substance of a bill during the legislative process so that both may be scrutinized by an appropriate committee.

(x) A joint House-Senate Committee on Economic Policy, co-chaired by a government and opposition member, be created to hold pre-budget hearings at which the Minister of Finance, the Governor of the Bank of Canada, the President of the Treasury Board and other witnesses as it desires, appear and which also receives and scrutinizes the Annual Report of the Economic Council of Canada.

(xi) A standing committee be created to examine the finances of selected crown corporations each year.

(xii) A standing committee on the government expenditures be struck to receive and examine a White Paper on expenditures which the government must present to parliament early in the session, before the publication of the estimates, and which should contain information on expenditure plans and projections for a three-year period on a department and program basis.

(xv) Standing committees be given the power to decide what they want to investigate within their jurisdiction.

(xvi) Both the government and the opposition loosen the rules of discipline with respect to voting by individual members on committees and that the definition of what constitutes a vote of confidence in the government be redefined.

Other reform proposals for the operation of the House of Commons and the committees have been put forward: some are more detailed, others less. But regardless of what is suggested, the need for reform of the legislative process, if we are to have responsible government in Canada, seems clear. Not all are sanguine that reform would achieve as much as proponents suggest, but most think reform is essential.[17]

Given the general agreement that reform is necessary, why does it not take place? There are a variety of reasons. All large institutions are difficult to change and Parliament is no exception. Moreover, its long history and its traditions make resistance to change strong. No one is certain in advance precisely what reform will bring and therefore all reform is looked upon with trepidation. Often strong and influential members think the system that was adequate when they were first elected is still adequate. Reform will require long and arduous debate because there will never be agreement as to the form the reform should take.

However, by far the biggest obstacle to change is the fact that the government in power, regardless of the party, knows that the system as it is now designed favours the executive, and given the pressures on a government to deal with current matters — inflation, energy, unemployment, social welfare, and so on — parliamentary reform simply does not receive high priority. Indeed, the committee system development in 1968 took place not because the government particularly wanted it but rather because it could not get its legislative package enacted under the existing rules. Unless there are compelling reasons to act on reform, it is unlikely that any government will do much to make Parliament more effective.

There are, however, a number of things that can be done that might make it imperative for the government to act. First, an individual M.P. working constantly, continuously, and cleverly, using all the rules of the House and committees and every available avenue for publicity, can, through perseverance, make an issue so significant that it cannot be ignored by the government. The classic example of this strategy in Canada is the experience of Jed Baldwin, M.P. for Peace River, and one-time House Leader of the Progressive Conservative Party, who single-handedly created the pressure for freedom of information legislation in Canada. He convinced his own party to accept the principle, and the Clark government announced in its Speech from the Throne that it would introduce a freedom of information bill into Parliament. Following the Clark government, the Trudeau administration also promised freedom of information legislation. The fact is Baldwin developed such a constituency for the idea among members and the media that no administration could avoid introducing it, even though there was never enthusiasm for such legislation among members of the government and even less — substantially less — among the public service. Baldwin demonstrated what one man could do in spite of strong Cabinet and bureaucratic resistance.

Second, an issue may be made so important to the public that the government cannot refuse to act on it. Occasionally, despite great public pressure, such as in the case of capital punishment, members do not seem to reflect the will of the public, but in most instances legislators want to do what the public wants. They want to be good representatives. If an issue becomes of significant enough importance to the public, Parliament will act. The problem is that the public is not easily excited about parliamentary reform and therefore it is difficult to mount sufficient public demand to make action imperative.

Third, a group of M.P.'s can create sufficient interest within a party for reform and then a party can take the issue to the public. To some degree this happened in the 1979 campaign when reform of Parliament was one of the issues developed by Clark and, to the amazement of many professional politicians, became a matter of some concern to some of the public. The proposals advanced by Clark involved changes in the way in which the estimates would be examined and more power for opposition members in committee.

The reports of the Auditor General also have considerable impact on public opinion, and if the Auditor General is a crusader for change he can have influence. Indeed, it was pressure from the Auditor General, who reported that the financial controls of the federal government were far below acceptable standards, that led to the creation of the Royal Commission on Financial Management and Accountability, which has recommended fundamental changes in the administration and the responsibility of sectors of the government, and which also calls for important parliamentary reform.

In the last analysis, however, once pressure is created for change, it will only come about if the pressure is channelled by Members of Parliament. Moreover, given the way the system operates, the members who will force change are likely to be those that do not see themselves as professional politicians and who indeed may not even have ambition to be in the Cabinet, but who are determined to see Parliament play a more influential role in the governing of the country.

The problem in Parliament is that there is deep confusion between form and substance. Committees meet and therefore it is presumed they are effective; question period is colourful and therefore it is assumed that it is a useful way to extract information from the government; speeches are made because so many days are allocated for a bill and it is believed that they are relevant. The fact is that in spite of a tremendous increase in the expenditure of taxpayers' funds, Parliament is not as effective an institution as it should and could be in terms of what it is supposed to do. If the first task of each committee of Parliament was to cost its operations, there would be horror expressed from coast to coast when that cost was assessed against the results of most committee hearings.

Mr. Stanfield's proposal[18] that control will be gained by Parliament doing less is interesting but not realistic. Control will be regained when there is a body of parliamentarians either with or without the support of their party who insist that the structure and rules of Parliament be changed so that they can be effective members.

If a Member of Parliament is able to make an input in a meaningful way into legislation through, for example, serving on a committee with real powers to modify, change, and improve legislation, it is not impossible that more people who do not want to make a lifetime career in politics could be induced to seek elective office. The presence of such experts in the House and on committees could do much to improve the substantive nature of legislation.

Members of Parliament are always busy, but too much of the time they are busy doing nothing — attending meaningless meetings, listening to inconsequential speeches. With the problems always facing the nation, clearly a top priority of any legislative body should be to make itself relevant so that it can contribute to the solution of the issues, which is what its members are elected and expected to do.

As one CEO put it, "reform of the policy-making process in Canada is far more critical to the future of the country than anything, including constitutional talks." Indeed, on both the executive and legislative side, reform is critical if the free society as we know it with responsible government is to survive. Businessmen with their under-standing of organizations and their task-oriented approach who enter politics can contribute much to the solution of this major problem in our society.

Political Parties and Policy Development

In the Canadian parliamentary system the role of political parties is crucial. It is the leader of the political party that elects the most Members of Parliament who forms the government and proposes the legislative programme. Consequently, the policies of the party are fundamental in determining the direction in which the nation will evolve, and the way in which the government will be administered.

The establishment of the policies of a political party is in one sense quite complex and in another quite simple. It is complex to the degree that all parties have policy conventions at which resolutions on the wide-ranging group of problems that a party must face are debated and adopted. Normally, a party has a policy committee with representation from local constituencies, party officials, and Members of Parliament, which presents the resolutions to the convention for approval. Occasionally, such resolutions are changed after debate, but normally what is placed before the convention is acceptable to the delegates, in no small measure because resolutions before presentation are given the imprimatur of the leader, and a major rejection of a policy position could be interpreted as a rejection of the leader. In an age of personality politics, this is a risk that few political parties are willing to run, particularly close to an election.

While the convention determines the major positions for a party, and it is important that business executives have an input into this party policy-setting process, Members of Parliament in the final analysis have greater impact on the general thrust of policy simply because once Parliament is in session, they must react on a daily basis to issues as they arise. However, all members do not have equal influence — their impact varies with their position and expertise.

In an opposition caucus the forces that determine the position that a party takes on a particular piece of legislation are primarily the following:

1. *The Position of the Leader* — Participatory democracy has not yet reached the major political parties in Canada. Leaders have enormous power. They determine the rate of advancement of members of the party, their popularity determines in many instances the ability of members to be elected, and they play a major role in the determination of policy. Obviously a successful leader must have his party and his members behind him on important policy initiatives, but his personal position on an issue can quite often be determinant.

2. *The Position of an Individual* — In any political caucus, individuals with expertise in particular matters are quickly identified. Most members do not have the background or experience to make a substantive judgement about many matters and they rely therefore

on the opinion of their colleagues. In the Progressive Conservative Party, for example, it is unlikely that a strong position taken on wheat by the Honourable Alvin Hamilton would be effectively challenged simply because it is recognized that Mr. Hamilton is an expert on the subject.

3. *The Make-Up of the Caucus* — The structure of the caucus in terms of urban-rural representation and geographic distribution impacts substantially on the nature of a decision. If a caucus has a large urban membership, consumer problems will take precedence over producer issues. A strong representation from one region, say Quebec or the West, will lead to positions that are most responsive to the needs of those areas.

4. *The Philosophy of the Party* — While there is a view that parties do not win or lose elections on issues, the basic philosophical position of a party, as it has developed through time, can and does affect the position taken by a party on a particular matter. There is no point, for example, of representatives of the energy industry trying to convince the N.D.P. caucus that a totally privately owned and operated energy industry is the most effective way to develop the energy resources of Canada.

5. *The Press* — The manner in which the press reports, analyses, and publicizes a position taken, or about to be taken, by a party has considerable influence on the nature of the decision simply because the public's opinion of a position may play a decisive role in an election.

6. *Politics* — Probably the most quoted aphorism of politicians is "You cannot do anything if you are not in power." Consequently, the political ramifications of a particular position are extremely important in the evolution of policy by a parliamentary caucus.

Politics is a constant task of reconciling opposing views. As someone once observed, "I can write an energy policy acceptable to Ontario before breakfast — lowest possible prices for consumers; and I can write one for Alberta in the same period of time — highest possible prices for producers. The difficulty is to write one for Canada." This need for compromise and for reconciliation of conflicting views are not normally the qualities of an effective businessman, and yet they are the skills that must be learned by the politician. The important point is that they can be learned relatively quickly and they are, in many instances, less important in terms of the general evolution of policy than substantive knowledge about a subject. In opposition, a new Member of Parliament can have impact on the development of policy positions relatively rapidly.

An opposition party within the present structure of the parliamentary system does not have much power. It can oppose, it cannot propose. Therefore, influencing the party does not often change what is happening in the nation. However, the goal of political parties is not to be in opposition but to be elected to power, and this does happen. The positions developed by the party when in opposition then become extremely important and do influence the nature of the policies brought into effect by the government. When the Clark government came to power in 1979, it had firm positions on freedom of information, assistance to home-owners through deduction of interest payments and real property tax in the calculation of personal income tax payments, energy (a shift from self-reliance to self-sufficiency), contraction of the public service, privatization of some Crown corporations, and changes in economic policy. These broad thrusts were developed primarily by caucus with some professional support and help from party members. Members of Parliament with expertise had a major role in their evolution.

Equally significantly, when the Clark government took office, in spite of opposition from public officials on part or all of these proposals, they moved ahead. They were part of the legislative package that the government planned to present to Parliament, as indicated in the Speech from the Throne. Indeed, the mortgage programme was contained in the budget of John Crosbie, the energy programme was negotiated with and agreed upon in principle by the producer provinces, the freedom of information legislation was in the process of preparation for presentation to Parliament, privatization committees were established, and the budget deficit would have been reduced by the Crosbie budget.

In opposition, therefore, indeed perhaps more in opposition than in government, the individual member can have a significant impact on the formulation of policy, which may become government policy, if he brings expertise to the job. There are always members of a caucus who are "professional politicians" who have chosen to make politics their career. They have an important input to make in policy determination — the politics of an issue — but they are not equipped, and know they are not equipped, to deal with many substantive issues and they do accept such input from any one who can bring it to the party. The impact of a seasoned executive in this process can be immense. No experienced executive should decline to enter the political process on the grounds that he will not have impact — the fact is that he will — if his party is in opposition, on the evolution of policy; and if his party is in power, probably in the administration of programmes.

The development of policy by a party in power is substantially more complex than by an opposition party. There are, of course, party conventions and party resolutions that set the major course of a party, but the exigencies of governing can alter that course very rapidly.

All of the factors that influence the evolution of policy in an opposition party are at work in the government party. The difference is that the government has the duty to propose legislation where the opposition is fundamentally opposing and monitoring.

In initiating legislation, there are so many additional forces that come into play, particularly the advice of the public service to the Cabinet and to the Prime Minister, that the role of the party member and the caucus may be less than in the case of the opposition. The opposition has no public service to provide it with expertise; the government does and the ministers use it. Consequently, the role of the expert in the government caucus is much less significant than in opposition. In fact, policy is usually not formulated in caucus, rather the "cabinet ministers attend caucus and provide information about pending government policy which serves as a foundation for caucus debate."[19] Moreover, the evolution of legislation is a long and arduous task. The original idea may be put forward many years before it surfaces through the bureaucracy in the form of a bill. Many members of the caucus might not even have been in Parliament when the government decided to go forward in a particular direction.[20] Finally, "the preeminence of the Prime Minister and cabinet exerts unarticulated psychological pressures on caucus members, even within their own jurisdiction . . ." and so "most of the time . . . the government can obtain, at minimum, acquiescence in its policies and in its schedule of business for the House."[21]

No Prime Minister can be effective, indeed survive, without the support of his caucus and therefore they normally try to work with their members. Issues are discussed at caucus, ministers do test positions with caucus members, and caucus members in turn bring forward their points of view. To the extent that it is done varies with individual ministers and the circumstances, but it is certainly the preferred method of proceeding.[22] It is probably true, however, that individual Members of Parliament in the government caucus have far less influence in determining policy of a party than do members of the opposition. On the other hand, a member of the government party may well be in the Cabinet or serve as a parliamentary secretary, and such positions are at the centre of the decision-making process. As a member of the government, a person has great influence and great power. It is not, of course, absolute — in a pluralistic society no one's power is — but it exists, and in spite of the change in the role of ministers in recent years, it is very real.

A businessman who is in the Cabinet can have influence on the ways in which the system of government evolves, on the machinery of government, on the nature of legislation, on the proclamation of rules and regulation, that no one outside of the system can match. The degree of power by an individual member of Cabinet depends on many factors: his political base, his relationship with the Prime Minister, his portfolio, his dealing with the public service, and his general parliamentary and political skills.

The skills brought by the business executive to government administration are precisely the skills that the task requires. A Cabinet minister, above all, must be able to absorb information, order facts, and make decisions. In addition, he must be able to manage his time, his department, and his officials. The businessman knows how to do these things, and it makes him extremely effective in the process of governing.

In either situation, opposition or government, the elected representative does have influence in determining policy. The amount varies in different circumstances and depends upon the skills and attributes of the person. But it is real and no one should reject entering the political arena on the grounds that under the system it is impossible to have any impact. Indeed, there is no other way to have as much impact. If business executives want to modify the direction in which the nation is moving, they must realize this and become more involved in the political process.

Being a Businessman and Getting Elected

It is all very well to make the case for businessmen in Parliament, but no matter how many chief executive officers accept nomination, before they can have any impact on policy they must get elected. In spite of the fact that businessmen such as C.D. Howe, Walter Gordon, and Robert Winters, to name a few, had very successful political careers and great impact on the nation, it is still contended by many that it is impossible for businessmen to get elected. This belief is reinforced by the fact that there are few businessmen from large organizations in the House of Commons. But is this because businessmen are defeated in elections or is it because they do not stand for public office? In the 1979 and 1980 elections, few of the candidates could be classified as businessmen, and even fewer could be considered professional business managers, that is, directing corporations with five hundred or more employees. The proper explanation for the paucity of businessmen in the House is not that they cannot get elected, but rather that they do not try.

There is no lack of opportunity for businessmen to run for political office. Before every election both major parties in Canada actively seek candidates from business. The search for "name candidates" is almost as notorious in fact as it is in failure.

Businessmen reject the opportunity to run for elected office for many reasons. Among the most important are the following:

- The belief that because of public attitudes towards business, they cannot get elected
- The heavy financial sacrifice
- The disruption of family life
- The loss of position in the firm (when a businessman leaves his position he must be replaced, and many feel that when they return to the firm they will be given positions of responsibility far junior to those that will be held by their current contemporaries who have never left the company)
- The public scrutiny of their actions and activities
- The belief that they will not have any real influence on important issues
- The widely held view that politics is not an attractive profession
- The development of strong "conflict of interest" legislation that may require them to divest holdings and prevent them from returning to their previous business activities.

Most of these reasons for declining to seek nomination are raised by all potential candidates. It is true, however, that peer group pressure against politicians is probably greater in business than in other occupations; and that it is more difficult to resume a professional career in business after a term as an elected politician than in some other activities, notably the practice of law. And, of course, for all but those fortunate few who represent constituencies in and around Ottawa, the wear and tear of elected office on life-style is inescapable. If a member decides to live in Ottawa, he is constantly travelling to his riding; but if he lives in the riding, he is away much of the time from Ottawa. Since parliamentary sessions often last eleven months, regardless of which choice is made, the impact on a member's personal life is profound.[23]

Once having decided to seek election, what must the business executive do to win? In the first place he must, as anyone else, choose his constituency with care. A farmer will have considerable difficulty in getting elected in an urban riding, an Anglophone will not win in Quebec City, and an ethnic will not win in a non-ethnic riding and vice versa. White, Anglo-Saxon Protestants have the best chance of victory in white Anglo-Saxon Protestant ridings.[24]

It is fundamental that the assets of the candidate match as closely as possible the perceptions of what the electorate want in a Member of Parliament. Normally business executives do best in constituencies where the average income is high, the number of voters with university and post-graduate degrees is large, and where a high proportion of the voters are employed in managing business, the professions, or own their own enterprise. It is also important to assess the number of votes that have to be turned around when an incumbent is running. The fewer votes that have to be changed, the more likelihood of victory.[25]

Most businessmen asked by a political party to stand for election have some choice, in urban areas, where they wish to run. But the freedom of choice is not unlimited. Sitting members who wish to stand again usually have the first choice for the nomination; defeated candidates if they are still interested may lay a claim to the nomination.[26] Riding associations sometimes have someone in mind; the party headquarters may, and usually does, have views on who are good candidates; and nominations can, of course, be contested. No one, therefore, has a guarantee that he can run wherever he wants, but on the other hand there is no point in a person running where he cannot get elected.

Under the constitution of most Canadian political parties, it is the responsibility of local riding associations to seek candidates to stand for election and to arrange nomination meetings, unlike in Great Britain, where candidates are often selected by the national party and allocated to various ridings. Occasionally, the national headquarters of a party will attempt to move someone into a particular riding, but "parachuting" seldom works for the candidate, and it will never work if the local riding association is opposed to the choice.

Nominations are often contested, particularly when it appears that the party will form the government. For anyone seeking elected office the first time, a contested nomination is a good thing. It makes the candidate better known; it requires some organization, and it can be the beginning thrust in an election campaign. Moreover, it is a good test of a candidate's capacity as a politician: if he cannot win a contested nomination he cannot win an election.

For a newcomer in politics, it is important to hold the nomination well before an election is called so that he can become known in the riding and plan the campaign well before it actually starts. It is very important for a candidate, particularly a newcomer to politics, to have the riding association's support because the members of the association have wide knowledge of the constituency, experience in campaigning, and a great desire to work in elections. Candidates normally have their own supporters and workers and it is important to meld the two groups together, the old and the new, to fight a winning campaign.

Elections cost money but financing is no longer a critical issue. Under the election law, expenditures in ridings are limited to $1 each for the first 15,000 names appearing on the voters list, $0.50 for the next 10,000, and $0.25 each for the rest, and for most businessmen candidates it is not difficult to raise the maximum amount that may be spent.[27]

It is important to develop a strategy and in doing so it is essential to remember that in politics a first principle is reality. A person cannot be something other than he is. For the businessman, this means that he must run as a businessman and this is not necessarily bad. The fact is that the electorate wants Members of Parliament who can manage the nation's business. They want people who can deal with issues, and when the issues are primarily associated with the economy, the experienced businessman is running from strength.

It is impossible to over-estimate the importance of organization in any election campaign. Regardless of television and the newspapers, the key to victory, even in urban areas, is canvassing the electorate — both by workers and the candidate.[28] And this can only be done properly through organization. It is a function of planning, staffing, directing, and controlling — all things that a businessman should do well.

Advertising campaigns, sign campaigns, special interest (youth, senior citizens, and so forth) campaigns, and election-day operations all have to be put into play. Special events are important, such as all-candidates meetings,[29] and need to be planned. Policy positions have to be articulated and refined. It is a full-time strenuous activity to run in an election.

There is no guarantee of winning, but there is little evidence that being a businessman is a negative factor in the electoral process. It is important that any businessman who seeks office pick where he runs with care, look upon his business experience as a positive factor, and use his management talents in the election process. He should not worry if a nomination is contested and he should use the local riding association in every way possible. He should also bring in his friends and associates to help in the campaign, particularly those with special talent in publicity and organization. And above all, he should exploit the fact that he is knowledgeable about and knows how to deal with the major problems of the day, simply because he has had business and management experience.

While it is clear that the power of the legislature in Canada at the present time is weak and that it performs its functions ineffectively, it is only through the political process that fundamental change in policy direction can be made. This means that if they want change, members of the private sector must become more involved in the process, and the most effective way of doing so is to become directly involved in politics. Businessmen can be and are elected, and history has demonstrated that they can be extremely influential forces in government. Indeed, Walter Gordon, alone, probably shaped the direction of more Canadian economic policy because he was active in politics (and in spite of the fact that he had serious difficulties when he was Minister of Finance) than all senior corporate officials who never entered politics put together. Because of Gordon, there is the Canada Development Corporation, the Foreign Investment Review Agency, the Carter tax reforms, and the auto-pact. Businessmen who believe these changes are wrong for the economy should reflect on how important entering the political process can be for the formulation of policy.

In a pluralistic society operating under the "consent doctrine," all sectors must be represented if the system is to work well. The best hope for the private sector influencing major policy in the nation surely lies in increased political participation by businessmen in the electoral process.

Notes

[1] The influence of the Senate, except in a small number of special situations, is very limited.

[2] There is imbalance in the House of Commons in terms of representation by occupation. The House is dominated by lawyers. In 1970, in the 28th Parliament, out of a total of 265 members, 71 were lawyers and 14 of the 29 members of the Cabinet were also lawyers. In 1979, 60 were lawyers, and 14 members of the Cabinet of 31 were lawyers. Only 2 Cabinet members had had major large business experience and only 6 had had any business experience of any kind.

[3] W.M. Lee, "Business-Government — A Case for Involvement," Speech delivered to the Board of Trade, Ottawa, October 1971, p. 7.

[4] Alex Jupp, "A Tyro MP Collides with 'the Process'," *Executive* 22 (May 1980), pp. 47–48.

[5] Of the sixteen Prime Ministers of Canada, none have been primarily businessmen.

[6] Royal Commission of Financial Management and Accountability, *Final Report* (Ottawa: Minister of Supply and Services Canada, 1979), p. 371.

[7] *Ibid.*, p. 370.

[8] Michael Rush, "The Development of the Committee System in the Canadian House of Commons — Diagnosis and Revitalization," *The Parliamentarian* 55 (April 1974), p. 91.

[9] Committees are not able to change the substance of legislation — only to recommend improvements in the manner in which it is enacted.

[10] C.E.S. Franks, "The Dilemma of the Standing Committees of the Canadian House of Commons," *Canadian Journal of Political Science* 4 (December 1971), p. 470.

[11] John M. Reid, "The Backbencher and the Discharge of Legislative Responsibilities," in *The Legislative Process in Canada: The Need for Reform*, edited by W.A.W. Neilson and J.C. MacPherson (Montreal: The Institute for Research on Public Policy, 1978), p. 140.

[12] Donald C. Macdonald, "Comments" on J. M. Reid, "The Backbencher and the Discharge of Legislative Responsibilities," in *The Legislative Process in Canada: The Need for Reform*, edited by W.A.W. Neilson and J.C. MacPherson (Montreal: The Institute for Research on Public Policy, 1978), p. 154.

[13] Paul G. Thomas, "Comments" on J.M. Reid, "The Backbencher and the Discharge of Legislative Responsibilities," in *The Legislative Process in Canada: The Need for Reform*, edited by W.A.W. Neilson and J.C. MacPherson (Montreal: The Institute for Research on Public Policy, 1978), p. 155.

¹⁴ Quoted in John B. Stewart, *The Canadian House of Commons: Procedure and Reform* (Montreal: McGill-Queen's University Press, 1977), p. 178.

¹⁵ Robert M. MacIntosh, "The Role of Business in Public Policy," Remarks delivered to the Institute of Management Consultants of Ontario, Toronto, 14 May 1979, p. 8.

¹⁶ Thomas d'Aquino, G. Bruce Doern, and Cassandra Blair, *Parliamentary Government in Canada: A Critical Assessment and Suggestions for Change*, study prepared for the Business Council on National Issues (Ottawa: Intercounsel, 1979), pp. 5–14.

¹⁷ J.A.A. Lovink, "Parliamentary Reform and Governmental Effectiveness in Canada," *Canadian Public Administration* 16 (Spring 1973), pp. 52–54.

¹⁸ Robert L. Stanfield, "The Present State of the Legislative Process in Canada: Myths and Realities," in *The Legislative Process in Canada: The Need for Reform*, edited by W.A.W. Neilson and J.C. MacPherson (Montreal: The Institute for Research on Public Policy, 1978), p. 47.

¹⁹ R.J. Jackson and M.M. Atkinson, "The Government's Legislative Programme and Its Linkage to Parliament," in *Apex of Power: The Prime Minister and Political Leadership in Canada*, 2d ed., edited by T. Hockin (Scarborough: Prentice-Hall, 1977), p. 242.

²⁰ See, for example, Prime Minister Trudeau's discussion of the development of Indian policy in "Pierre Trudeau on Policy-Making and the Growth of the Prime Minister's Office Since 1968," in *Apex of Power: The Prime Minister and Political Leadership in Canada*, 2d ed., edited by T. Hockin (Scarborough: Prentice-Hall, 1977), p. 268.

²¹ Jackson and Atkinson, *op. cit.*, p. 242.

²² Pierre Trudeau, "The Prime Minister and the Parliamentary Caucus," in *The Apex of Power: The Prime Minister and Political Leadership in Canada*, 2d ed., edited by T. Hockin (Scarborough: Prentice-Hall, 1977), pp. 151–53. The Honourable Alvin Hamilton often states that he found attending caucus one of the more difficult tasks in his experience as a Cabinet minister, simply because the caucus was so involved and articulate about the actions which he took in his departments.

²³ Parliament itself could do much to alleviate some of these problems. At the moment there is no specified calendar for parliamentary activities: no starting date, no specified time for recesses, no date for closing. The result is that members have no control over their time in terms of planning vacations or time with their constituents. Every year a calendar is suggested — usually that Parliament commence on the day after Labour Day, rise for two weeks at Christmas, return on January 2, and adjourn at the end of June. No government ever wishes to propose legislation for regularizing the sitting of the House of Commons and the Senate because it feels the threat of keeping Parliament in session gives it additional power in getting legislation passed.

²⁴ The importance of choosing the proper riding cannot be over-estimated. For example, when Ronald Ritchie, a Vice-President of Imperial Oil with a long record of activity in public affairs, decided to seek election in 1974, he chose to run for the Progressive Conservative nomination in Wellington. His reasoning was that (1) he had been the Chairman of the Board of Governors of the University of Guelph and Guelph is the principal centre of population in Wellington and so he felt he would be reasonably well known there; and (2) the constituency had been held for the Progressive Conservative Party by Mr. Alfred Hales for many years and he was retiring. Ritchie expected his support, but in a highly contested nomination such support was not as influential as Ritchie expected it to be, and it turned out that Ritchie was not as widely known in the community as he had supposed. He lost that nomination but subsequently ran for the Progressive Conservative Party, as a service to the party, in Algoma, a traditional rural Liberal riding, where he was defeated. However, in 1979 he ran and won in East York in Metropolitan Toronto.

One should never over-estimate — unless one is an entertainer or professional athlete — how well he is known in the community. When I sought the nomination for the Progressive Conservative Party in Don Valley, I had been an active Dean of a

Faculty of Administrative Studies, on the Board of the Metropolitan Zoo, on a hospital board, on the board of several companies, an active speaker, and I wrote a weekly column that appeared in the *Toronto Daily Star*. When we ran a recognition survey of me in the constituency, I was known by less than one per cent of the voters.

25 This is not always easy to estimate. For example, in 1972 when I ran in Don Valley, the majority of votes that had to be changed was the lowest in the ridings in that part of Toronto. However, it was difficult to know whether this was because Robert Kaplan who held the riding was new in 1968 and he ran against the ever-present Dalton Camp who at that time was popular in Toronto, although not popular enough to get elected, for working to remove Mr. Diefenbaker as leader of the Progressive Conservative Party.

26 Sometimes this problem can be exacerbated when a previous candidate cannot make up his mind whether he wants to run or not. In 1972 in Don Valley, in spite of repeated protestations of having no interest in the nomination, after I had decided to run, Dalton Camp changed his mind and suggested that in fact he might like to run — at least he would like the nomination meeting delayed. He did not hold to this position when I informed him that I would challenge the nomination.

27 The 1972 campaign in Don Valley set a record for the most money ever spent in a constituency. It is estimated that each candidate spent more than $75,000. It is wise for a candidate to take the position that he will not spend his own money in a campaign. There are many examples where in the heat of an election a contestant believes that an extra few thousand dollars will mean the difference between victory and defeat and goes into debt to raise the money. There is nothing more difficult to do than raise money after an election for a candidate — particularly one who has lost. A good principle to follow is that if a candidate puts forward his time and energy and commitments, he should not put forward his money. Moreover, the extent that others finance the campaign is an indication of the strength of support. Regardless of one's personal circumstances, a candidate should not finance his own election.

28 There can never be too many workers in a campaign. If a volunteer is told there is nothing that has to be done then the campaign is not properly organized. Canvassers are always needed. In the 1972 and 1974 campaigns, I knocked on 15,000 and 12,000 doors respectively. The reception was always warm, and I am convinced that any person who does not have a strong commitment to a party will vote for a candidate whom he meets.

29 Each constituency develops its own election traditions. In most metropolitan ridings where it is likely that a businessman would run, "all-candidates meetings" are important. At such meetings electors want to find out where a candidate stands on various issues. The key to success at such events is to be clear and unequivocal. Voters will often support a candidate with whom they disagree on a particular issue, but they will seldom support one who equivocates about significant matters.

Towards a New Congruence: The Future of the Private Sector in Canada

8

In the 1970s, the influence of the private sector in the determination of the public interest and the establishment of public policy decreased substantially in Canada. It is not astonishing, therefore, that during the period, programmes were put into effect that business felt were inappropriate and the alienation of the private from the public sector increased dramatically. The decline in the influence of business was not the result of some plot or plan on the part of government, but the perfectly predictable consequence of corporations using strategies in dealing with government that were out of date and ineffective. Moreover, it is certain that if corporate strategies do not change, the influence of the private sector in the formulation of public policies will continue to decline and the proportion of goods and services produced by the public sector will undoubtedly increase. In turn, this will lead to even more alienation of business from government in the years ahead.

Clearly, this is a development that no one wants. In a pluralistic democracy, it is not healthy for any major sector of society to be alienated from government — not good for government, not good for the sector, and not good for the majority of citizens. After all, as one CEO has written, "government is put there by all the people and that includes business leaders and people involved in business, in order to help all of us to live together in an ordered way. . . ." It is to everyone's advantage for the differences between business and government — differences so great that Prime Minister Trudeau described the relationship in 1981 as "the new Canadian two solitudes" [1] — to be reconciled as much as possible. The question is, How can this be done?

Several years ago when I was a young professor on the faculty of the Graduate School of Management at UCLA, I was walking across the campus with Franklin Murphy, then Chancellor and CEO of the university and more recently chairman of the board of the Los Angeles Times Corporation. Dr. Murphy had shortly before arrived at UCLA from the University of Kansas and we had been attending a particularly difficult meeting among faculty, students, and administrators. I commented to Murphy that at moments like these he must wish that he had never left Kansas, to which he replied, "Jim, never look back." He did not mean, of course, that we cannot learn from the past but that we cannot duplicate it and we should not spend too much of our effort trying.

Murphy's maxim, while not particularly profound, is relevant to the Canadian CEO. The fact is that the environment within which the Canadian corporation is operating in the 1980s is substantially different than it was in the 1950s and 1960s, and consequently the methods for dealing with government that were appropriate in that period are not, and should not be expected to be, appropriate in the 1980s and 1990s. The growth of government has led to a more complex system of policy making; an increase in affluence has led to shifts in influence among various groups; and changes in the value system of society have led to less automatic acceptance of the role of any institution, including the corporation, in society.

In addition, in the 1950s and early 1960s, consensus among the decision makers in the public and private sectors on the optimum methods of achieving the economic goals of society was reasonably easy to achieve, primarily because their backgrounds and value systems were similar. By the 1980s, in a more complex world with a different system of decision making and with new decision makers in government, this was no longer necessarily true, and so, no matter how hard they tried, by the mid-1970s it was impossible for CEOs to have the same type of close, personal, intimate, and influential relationships with the key public-sector decision makers as existed during the post-war period.

Despite all these changes, more than half of the CEOs and directors of major Canadian corporations still believed in 1980 that the methods used in the 1950s were the most effective for influencing the development of public policy. Naturally, their influence has dropped — and it will continue to decrease — until they begin to develop and use management strategies for dealing with government based on the realities of the next decades. The 1950s are over and they are not coming back. C.D. Howe is really dead.

There are some — in both the public and the private sectors — who believe that the rupture between business and government has become so great that nothing can be done to reconcile the differences in anything more than a marginal manner. This can only be true, however, if over the past two decades the goals of the corporation and the public interest have become so different that the corporation, which exists at the sufferance of the state, no longer has, or is no longer perceived to have, an important role to play in the economy.

But has this happened? Have the changes in the Canadian economy and the processes of government been so great that the collective goals of the private sector and governments are completely opposite? Is the situation in the 1980s that much different from the 1950s, when it was generally agreed that the economic goals of the public and the private sectors were essentially the same and that the most effective way for the public interest to be fulfilled was by the sectors working together?

All evidence indicates that the answer to these questions is no. The central economic objective of society is to have full employment with relatively stable prices, a just and reasonable welfare system, opportunities for personal growth and progress, effective control of the economy by Canadians, less regional disparities in income, and a fair sharing of the cost of government. There are, as there always will be, differences of views between levels of governments and between governments and the private sector about which goals are most important, and the priority that should be assigned to their fulfilment; but by and large the economic goals of governments and the goals of the private sector are the same. Indeed, at the beginning of the 1980s, there was probably as much congruence between the goals of the corporation and the goals of society as in any period in the last two decades. Certainly they were closer than they had been during the period of social unrest and change in the late 1960s and early 1970s.

The major difference between the sectors — and the one most difficult to reconcile — revolves not around goals, but on how the goals can best be achieved. There are those who argue that a viable economy can only be attained through more activity on the part of government; others believe that the most effective method for achieving economic goals is through a stronger private sector. This difference, while perhaps much more pronounced at the beginning of the 1980s than in the past, has always been present and it has always been resolved in Canada in a very pragmatic fashion. The decision on how the production of goods and services should be organized, in the private or the public sector, has never been made on ideological grounds but rather by more or less mutual agreement by all concerned on the most efficient way of getting something done. Such agreement was forged from the input of all sectors affected by the decision, and in this way, through the years, the public and private sectors were able to function together successfully in what has come to be known as a "mixed economy."

The only way the system can work, however, is for all sectors to have influence in the decision-making process. Because recent methods used by the private sector for making an input into the determination of public policy have not been effective, one of the sectors that is most directly affected by policy decisions about the economy is not participating in their determination. In a very real sense, therefore, a basic tenet of the consent doctrine of government, that is, that those who are governed must have an input into the determination of the public policy that impacts upon them, has not been maintained. However, this does not mean that there are irreconcilable differences between the public and private sectors, that the mixed economy concept must be jettisoned, but only that the reconciliation process for assuring co-operation between the sectors is not working well.

Given this situation, it is clear that one of the most important tasks of CEOs in the 1980s must be the development of strategies that permit the private sector once again to have meaningful input in the determination of the public interest. If this is to be done successfully, then many of the assumptions and practices that have dominated business-government relations over the past years must be discarded.

First, it must be recognized that the corporation is no longer automatically granted a special place in society, which makes its defence unnecessary. The capacity of the corporation to contribute to the public interest is not automatically accepted — it must be demonstrated and explained. Indeed, in some industries, assessing, reacting to, and influencing public policy decisions may mean the difference not only between short-term success or failure of the enterprise, but between the survival or non-survival of the firm. The nationalization of asbestos, potash, and parts of the energy industry in recent years is evidence of this fact. Chief executive officers have to accept the responsibility, because no one else has the capacity or ability to do so, of convincing the Canadian public and the Canadian government of the significant role that the private sector should play in the economy, and the conditions necessary for its effective functioning. Even though CEOs neither like nor feel particularly well equipped to fulfil this formidable function, they or their senior executives no longer have the luxury of avoiding it.

The argument that it is the task of the businessman to supply the goods and services that society wants, and the duty of the political system to establish the conditions under which the economic system operates — and that there is a sharp dichotomy between the two — is no longer, if it ever was, sustainable.[2] It is an important responsibility and, under the consent doctrine, duty of businessmen to contribute to the formulation of the conditions under which business operates, to be involved in the establishing of the public purpose and determining how it will be fulfilled. Obviously, businessmen should neither expect, nor want, the public interest to be determined by businessmen alone, just as no one in society should either want or expect public policy to be evolved without the input of those who understand how the private sector operates. It is a question of balance.

Second, the planning and execution of an effective business-government relations strategy must become a highly professional activity. It can no longer be limited to *ad hoc* reactions and hurried trips to the national or provincial capitals to meet the appropriate minister or official. Corporate management must understand how governments make decisions, the changing role of various agencies and institutions in the country, the increase and decrease of the influence of people, and the nature and the reasons for the public's different perception of the corporation. They must devise corporate strategies that are pro-active and include political action, public debates, massive educational programmes, advocacy advertising, and other activities and costs that many corporations have assiduously avoided. And all these things must be done, if they are to be effective, in a highly professional manner.

Third, given the great significance of business-government relations and the strategies that must of necessity be employed, the training and preparation for the position of CEO in many industries must be quite different than it has been in the past. The time is fast approaching, if it has not already arrived, when the CEO must truly be a public figure, able to deal as competently with the media, government, special interest groups, and other external forces that impinge both directly and indirectly on the firm, as he had dealt with traditional management functions in the past. Indeed, experience in elected office or in government administration may be as effective preparation for the future CEO as additional time in yet another division of the corporation. Wise boards of directors in many industries are grooming people with this type of talent within their organizations, or are attracting them to their companies, for future senior positions.

Fourth, it is imperative that there be more direct input into the policy decision-making process by people who understand how the private sector works and the contribution that it can make to the economy. Such input has to come not through influence — which is always difficult to measure and always ephemeral — but from direct participation. There must be more people with senior executive experience in the decision-making process of government. Individual CEOs, speaking from their position as CEOs, can have some influence on public opinion, but the basic explanation and defence of the enterprise system, as a system, must come from people who have the legitimacy of election as a basis for their views. In short, more CEOs must enter public life. Robert Winters, if he had remained in the business community, would undoubtedly have expressed the same ideas that he did as a minister of the Crown. It would not have mattered. To have decisive impact, one must be in the decision-making process.

Obviously all business managers are not frustrated politicians and few will ever be involved in elected politics; and it is naïve to argue that the presence of a few more people in the policy decision-making group from the private sector is going to change radically the direction of government in the nation. But it is equally naïve to believe that they would not have significant impact. Canada has traditionally been governed by strong individuals who have had a vision of the nation, of the governmental process, and of the appropriate role of the various sectors of society. They made a difference. Canada is a different nation because Pierre Trudeau had been Prime Minister during the 1970s than it would have been if David Lewis had been in power; and different than if Robert Winters had replaced Lester Pearson as Prime Minister rather than Mr. Trudeau; and different than if the Prime Minister had been Walter Gordon. Whether the government would have achieved its goals more effectively, indeed what the goals of government would have been under the different men, is not the point. What is important is that the nation would have been different. The significance of individuals in the system should not be under-estimated.

This change in business-government strategy from a private to a public approach is based on the reality that neither businessmen nor the representatives of any sector of society will be able in the 1980s, or indeed the forseeable future, to make an effective input into the determination of the public interest without being publicly involved in public debate about public issues. Business, like all groups in society, will have to make its case in the arena of public opinion — not in the ministers' offices.

On many occasions the strategies used by business in dealing with government may be extremely adversarial, but this does not mean that they cannot be constructive and effective. Chief executive officers dislike adversarial tactics — most people do — but adversarial approaches are both inevitable and acceptable in the Canadian form of government. The parliamentary system is the ultimate adversarial type of government, and in a free society the public interest is determined through the accommodation by the political process — normally after vigorous debate — of the interests of various and usually opposing sectors of society.

It would be a great mistake to believe that business-government relations are failing in the 1980s if they become more adversarial. Indeed, the contrary will be true. If the relationship is not more adversarial, it will be ineffective. And if it is ineffective, the role of the private sector in the economy will decline, and the alienation of business from government instead of diminishing will increase.

Such an approach is very different from those that have been traditionally used and that are based on the belief that it is the purpose of business-government strategies to maintain harmony between the goals of a business, or industry, and the public purpose, when the public purpose is expressed in government policy. Important as harmony may be, it is not as important as survival. Obviously it is impossible to have harmony in goals if the goal of the public policy is to nationalize the firm. Future emphasis in corporate strategy must be on influencing the formulation of public policy to assure that the private sector will continue to play a significant role in the Canadian economy — not on reacting to public decisions and attempting to maintain a harmony of purpose when such a harmony is clearly adverse to the private sector.

There are two sides to the business-government relationship, and while business is evolving new strategies for having effective input into the determination of the public interest, changes will also be occurring in the operation of governments. Evidence indicates that the machinery of government at the federal level is not working well, that the executive branch of the government is having difficulty in making and implementing its decisions. Clearly, the system must be opened up by constantly bringing into government people from outside the system, particularly people with management experience and training. And most importantly, if the relationship between the private and the public sectors in the future is to achieve the heady success of the early post–World War II years, there must be a greater understanding among the senior members of government of the role that the private sector can play in a free society.

All these changes, important as they may be, pale to insignificance beside the major need — a need that must basically be fulfilled from the government side of the business-government equation, and that is the re-establishment of a formal, well-understood manner by which all sectors of society can have an input into the formulation of public policy. The most promising approach for doing so is through strengthening and reforming the legislature. Historically, because of the strong role played by the executive branch of government, the legislature has been relegated to a relatively passive part in the determination of policy. Consequently, it is not surprising that any group interested in influencing public policy has largely attempted to do so by relating to departments and public servants. They have realized that vital decisions have been made by the executive branch of government — the legislature has not mattered.

In the 1980s, however, when it is clear that the departments and the executive can no longer be as effective an avenue for the input of views as they once were, cannot the legislature begin to play a greater role in policy formulation, particularly in the great issues of our times? Indeed, is there any more appropriate place for effecting an accommodation among all the conflicting views of various segments of society than a committee of Parliament? Should not an appearance before a parliamentary committee become as effective a method for influencing the formulation of public policy as was a meeting with the appropriate Cabinet minister in 1950?

Before the legislature can play such a role, however, it must be reformed and the basic effort for reform must come from within the system. The need for major reform has passed from the realm of political theory to national necessity, and encouraging and assisting in every way possible those who are leading a reform movement must be central to all efforts to improve the relationship between government and business in Canada. It is the road to re-establishing what has been absent for almost a decade: an effective process whereby the sectors of society that are affected by impending policies can have some meaningful input into determining their nature — a fundamental requirement of government under the consent doctrine.

The prospects for Canada are unlimited. The resource wealth of the nation is unmatched by that of any other country; the social welfare system is superb; the level of education is outstanding. The opportunities for growth and prosperity for all Canadians have seldom, if ever, been greater.

What role will the private business sector play in assuring that these opportunities are seized? It could be large or it could be small; the decision is not yet made. What that decision will be depends upon the present and future CEOs of Canadian corporations and no one else. They have the Herculean task of (1) defining their responsibilities within their firms, their industries, and their country as including as a principal management function the task of explaining to all Canadians the positive role that the private sector is capable of playing in the fulfilment of the public interest; (2) participating themselves, or at least encouraging their peers to participate, in the public sector so that there is vigorous representation from the private sector in the determination of the public interest; and (3) operating their enterprises in such a fashion that the public interest, which they have had an input in determining, is achieved. If they do these things, the future of the corporation in Canada is secure; if they do not, the role of government in the economy will inexorably grow. The choice is ultimately theirs.

Notes

[1] In a speech to the Young Presidents Organization in Toronto, June 1981.

[2] For the most effective statement of this position, see Neil H. Jacoby, "Capitalism and Contemporary Social Problems," *Sloan Management Review* 12 (Winter 1971): 33–43.

Sources of
Information

Much of the information upon which this study is based was supplied
by eighty chief executive officers and/or directors of large publicly
owned private corporations, twenty former federal Cabinet ministers,
fourteen present or former executive officers of major trade associations, six professional business-government consultants, six people
with knowledge about some particular aspect of business-government
relations, and four journalists. Most answered a questionnaire and
supplemented their answers with extensive discussions of the issues.
Consequently, the study relies heavily on the assessments and
opinions of people who are, or have recently been, actively engaged in
or associated in some way with business-government activities.
Because the total number of people involved in this work in Canada is
not large, no attempt was made to draw a random sample of executive
officers of associations, large corporations' executives, or former
Cabinet ministers. Rather, efforts were directed to building on the
knowledge of the people directly involved. No statistical validity is
claimed for the results.

In 1979, the eighty CEOs and/or directors whose views are drawn
upon for this study were collectively directors of more than four
hundred Canadian corporations. The significance of these companies
in the Canadian economy is indicated in Table 1.

All answers to the questionnaires were received on a confidential
basis. However, to assist the reader in assessing the representative-
ness of the material, I am listing the names of the Cabinet ministers,
trade association officers, chief executive officers and directors, and
others, who provided information for the study. Seventy of the eighty
CEOs and/or directors answered every question; another ten did not
answer the questions directly, or answered only some of them, but
provided significant information pertaining to the questions.

Table 1

Financial Post 100 Largest Private (non-government corporations) in terms of Sales:	*Total Sales* $121.1 billion	*Reported** $76.5 billion
Financial Post 20 Largest Private (non-government corporations) Financial Institutions in terms of Assets:	*Total Assets* $21.0 billion	*Reported* $20.1 billion
Financial Post 20 Largest Private (non-government) Merchandisers in terms of Sales of Operating Revenue:	*Total Sales* $28.3 billion	*Reported* $11.4 billion
Financial Post 20 Largest Life Insurers in terms of Assets:	*Total Assets* $37.3 billion	*Reported* $29.7 billion
Financial Post 30 Big Subsidiaries (non-government owned):	*Total Assets* $12.0 billion	*Reported* $10.4 billion

* Sales or assets in 1979 of corporations of which either the CEO, one or more directors, or both are reported in this study.

Chief Executive Officers and Directors

Honourable John B. Aird
Donald Anderson
John A. Armstrong
Honourable James Balfour
Ralph Barford
Douglas G. Bassett
Thomas J. Bell
Roy F. Bennett
Conrad M. Black
James T. Black
William B. Boggs
E.C. Bovey
Charles R. Bronfman
James W. Burns
John B. Carmichael
Arthur J. Child
William A. Cochrane
Jacques Courtois
John B. Cronyn
Robert C. Dale
C. William Daniel
Paul Deacon
John S. Dewar
William A. Dimma
R.C. Dowsett
Gordon Fisher

Guy P. French
Donald Fullerton
George R. Gardiner
W. Douglas Gardiner
Reva Gerstein
Irving Gerstein
J. Douglas Gibson
Honourable John Godfrey
J. Peter Gordon
Gordon C. Gray
Sydney M. Hermant
Robert S. Hurlbut
Henry N.R. Jackman
Frederick W.P. Jones
Peter Kilburn
John D. Leitch
Arthur J. Little
Lorne K. Lodge
Frank H. Logan
W.A. Macdonald
Honourable Alan A. MacNaughton
Brian R.B. Magee
Honourable E.C. Manning
Alan R. Marchmant
Paul E. Martin
Brigadier Richard S. Malone

Darcy McKeough
W. Earle McLaughlin
Honourable Hartland Molson
John H. Moore
John H. Panabaker
John A. Pollock
Alfred Powis
John A. Rhind
Edward S. Rogers
Major-General Richard Rohmer
Murray G. Ross
Gordon R. Sharwood
Albert E. Shepherd
Arthur Smith

Honourable Richard Stanbury
J. Hugh Stevens
Robert A. Stevens
John L. Stoik
Maurice F. Strong
James C. Thackray
Richard M. Thomson
Douglas C. Trowell
William O. Twaits
J. Page Wadsworth
Stephen A. Wilgar
David B. Weldon
John H. White
Adam Zimmerman

Federal Cabinet Ministers

Honourable Ronald Atkey
Honourable Walter Baker
Honourable Perrin Beatty
Honourable David Crombie
Honourable John Crosby
Honourable Barnard Danson
Honourable Jacob Epp
Honourable John Fraser
Honourable Alvin Hamilton
Honourable William Jarvis

Honourable Otto Lang
Honourable Donald S. Macdonald
Honourable Elmer Mackay
Honourable James McGrath
Honourable Allan McKinnon
Honourable Mitchell Sharpe
Honourable Robert S. Stanbury
Honourable John N. Turner
Honourable Michael Wilson
Honourable John Wise

Executive Officers of Trade Associations

John L. Bonus
Donald J. Cruickshank
J. Foss
John E. Foy
Michael Harrison
Andrew G. Kniewasser
Kenneth R. Lavery

A.K. Maclaren
Keith B. McKerracher
Alasdair J. McKichan
David Morley
Robert Oliver
Ian Smyth
G.G.E. Steele

Others

Marshall Crowe
Thomas D'Aquino
J. Duncan Edmonds
Ralph Ferguson
Douglas Fisher
Walter Gray
J. Alex Jupp
Fraser Kelly

William M. Lee
Robert Logan
J. Albany Moore
William Neville
Val Sears
Jefferey Simpson
Torrance Wylie
John Yocum

Needless to say, the respondents, neither collectively nor individually, necessarily agree with the thrust of the study. In fact many disagree with some of the conclusions, some disagree with many of them, and a few disagree with all of them.

Questionnaire sent to CEOs and Directors

B

Some Leading Questions About the Relationships Between Politics, Government and Corporate Business

The following are some of the questions which seem to me to be relevant to an understanding of the relationships among politics, government, business and management. If you would please jot down your answers and return the sheet to me, I would very much appreciate it. The reason that I am not sending an all-embracing, normal type of questionnaire is that I believe this is an issue where qualitative views are as important as quantitative answers, interesting as the latter may be. So I do hope you will give me your general comments as well as answers to the questions below.

Politics-Personal:

Should senior executives of corporations be active in politics beyond the usual requirements of good citizenship?
Should they publicly endorse candidates for political office?
Should they publicly try to influence political decisions?
Should they take a more active role in political parties?
Should they publicly endorse legislation that is not directly concerned with their firm or industry?
Should businessmen appear before Committees of the House of Commons on legislation that is not directly concerned with their firm or industry?
Do you think businessmen, in general, are effective as politicians?
What is your view of the general quality of federal politicians?
Should more businessmen run for political office?

Politics-Corporation:

Do you think corporations should be politically active in issues that are not of direct concern to the firm or industry?
Should corporations publicly endorse positions before and/or during elections?

Should they attempt to influence public opinion through advertising about issues which are not of direct concern to the firm or industry?
Should they arrange for politicians to speak to employees?
Should they grant leaves of absence to employees to seek political office?
Should corporations invest in achieving a higher political profile?

General:

What are the most difficult problems facing business in attempting to influence government policy?
Do you think the fact that business is assumed to speak as a vested interest on all policy matters is fundamental to the problems between government and business?
Do you believe that much of the problem that business has in influencing policy arises from the difficulty business has in communicating its views to the government and to the public?
Do you think that Canadian business, in general, should take a more adversarial role with respect to the overall increase in government activity?
What do you think will be the most difficult government problems facing business in the next five years; for example, higher taxes, a stronger FIRA, more intervention in markets, etc.?
Do you think the climate for doing business in Canada during the next five years will improve, deteriorate, or remain about the same?

I am sure you may sense other issues that are much more pressing. I would be pleased if you would let me know about them as well. Thanks again.   *JG*.

Lessons
from Theory

C

There are many broad general theories about the state and the way it does, or should, relate to the economy. They range all the way from those of Adam Smith that businessmen when left alone to fulfil their personal interests are at the same time led by an invisible hand to promote an end (the public purpose), which is not part of their intention[1] to the economic determinism of Karl Marx, which asserts the virtues of socialism, and the analysis of Joseph Schumpeter, which concludes "that capitalism yields its place on the historical stage [to socialism] essentially for sociological reasons."[2]

From Smith has come the position of the Chicago school of economists and the rational choice school of the University of Virginia — that the best government is the least government. From Marx the thinking of the present-day social democrats has emerged, and in Schumpeter may be found the origins of some of the ideas of John Kenneth Galbraith as expressed in his concept of the new industrial state with the implications of such form of economic organization for public policy. In the writings of Lord Keynes, the person whose ideas have had the most sweeping impact in the thinking of policy makers in the Western industrialized world in the twentieth century, may be found traces of the work of both Smith and Marx.

While it may be interesting to be aware of the different interpretations and analyses of the forces shaping the nature of society, such concepts do not provide much assistance to the CEO seeking to find the reason why a particular policy has been adopted. He can, however, gain insight into the policy-making process from a study of some of the less general approaches that have been taken by contemporary scholars who analyse various aspects of public policy making. Indeed, anyone who wishes to have complete comprehension of the incredibly complex public decision-making process must be aware of the more important of these studies, and the conclusions that they reach.[3]

Organizing and Classifying

The organizational approach to interpreting policy formulation is demonstrated by Malcolm Taylor in his book *Health Insurance and*

Canadian Public Policy.[4] In this study, the best ever written about the evolution, development, and implementation of a public policy in Canada, Taylor uses a systems approach of organization and analysis, adopted largely from the early work of the American scholar David Easton.[5]

The analysis is done through asking and answering questions. First, Taylor asks: Why was a decision made? What were the constraints limiting the decision? What were the risks surrounding the choice? What were the contributions of external forces to the timing and content of the decision? The answers to these four questions identify the inputs into the decision-making process.

The fifth question focuses on the decision makers more directly. What was the contribution of the bureaucracy, government ministers, the Cabinet collectively, the caucus, legislature, and Parliament in the decision? The answer to this question identifies the within (inside) inputs into the policy formulation process. Taylor then asks: What kind of programme was created and how did the government introduce it? The answers give the outputs of the process. Finally, he analyses the results of the programme — the outcome.[6]

When taken all together, the inputs, withinputs, outputs, and outcome provide a closed system with a feedback loop that allows for a complete analysis of the ploicy-making process as it relates to the formulation and implementation of the health programme in Canada. Such an approach permits a definitive study of a specific policy, but it does not lend itself to generalization about all policy making. It may be, however, given the nature of public policy making, that classifying and analysing is the closest it is possible to come to identifying precisely how policy is established. It may not be a basis for theorizing, but it does provide a structured and organized insight into the policy-making process, and perhaps, when there are a greater number of detailed studies such as the type done by Professor Taylor, certain basic generalizations about public policy making can be drawn.

The Rational Decision Theory Approach

In the late 1950s and the 1960s, there was a belief in government that through the use of the policy sciences — the sciences that bridge the gap between "'a disjointed, partisan, incremental, consensus' view . . . [and] . . . a 'systematic, analytical, scientific, efficiency-oriented view'"[7] — the various techniques of information theory, programme planning and budgeting, management by objectives, and systems analysis could be used to achieve better policy decisions, better in the sense that the ramifications of decisions on a wide range of activities could be determined in advance of their implementation — something that had heretofore been impossible. Much has been written about this period of policy making in Canada and the conclusion of most studies is that the attempts, at that time, to bring "rational scientific policy processes" into the federal government did not succeed.[8]

A by-product of the failure of the effort, however, was the development of a theory of government policy making built around the concept of conflict resolution. According to this approach, there are no final theories of how government policy is made; that an understanding of decision making can only be gained by understanding how society resolves conflict — an understanding of process.[9] Clearly, a knowledge of conflict resolution is important for all managers, not only managers in government; but even more important is the need to identify the conflicts that matter. In major policy formulation, many are irrelevant and can be settled well down in the organizational structure without any impact whatsoever on the final policy outcome. Unfortunately, at this stage of development, the conflict resolution approach is of very little assistance in identifying those conflicts that matter from those that do not.

The Incrementalist Approach

One of the most ingenious and possibly the most accurate explanation of how policy is formulated by public servants was advanced in 1959. In a paper that is now considered a classic, entitled "The Science of 'Muddling Through'," G.E. Lindblom argues that regardless of any scientific measures or theories that may be proposed, an administrator in fact deals with what he can — and that means he chooses between policies that differ only in minor degree from policies that are now in effect. According to Lindblom, policies do not move by leaps and bounds, and this, he thinks, is a good thing.[10] It reduces possible alternatives and limits actions to the politically feasible, which in a democracy is essential. Moreover, policies that are not simply a minor extension, or increments, of existing policies are irrelevant because, he states, they cannot be implemented. He argues that it does not matter that certain impacts of a policy are neglected when an analysis is being made because if one agency of government ignores something, another agency will pick it up. If it is not looked after by someone, the issue that the policy ignores then problably does not need government attention. If it does, in our complex system where almost everything seems to be impacted by government, it is certain that some group will quickly go to work to correct any miscarriage of justice. Consequently, there is no particular reason, he states, to seek comprehensiveness in policies — something that is unattainable anyway.

"Making policy is at best a very rough process. Neither social scientists, nor politicians, nor public administrators yet know enough about the social world to avoid repeated error in predicting the consequences of policy moves."[11] According to Lindblom, the experienced administrator knows, therefore, that by proceeding through a series of additive decisions, he avoids the big jump that requires predictions which he cannot make, he avoids serious lasting mistakes, he tests his actions as he moves from one stage to another, and he remedies any errors relatively quickly. Naturally, this is the way an administrator wishes to operate, and because he prefers this "seat of the pants" approach, he is normally distrustful of theory and mistrusts theorists.[12] He also dislikes theories because most require more facts than the working administrator has available, or the resources to find, and normally they are so vague that they have no particular relevance. The value system applied to the policy process is largely that which the administrator brings with him to the policy-making process. Incrementalism, not theory, according to Lindblom, explains how policy is made.

Modern Theories and Understanding the Decision-Making Process

There are many additional explanations of policy formulation, but there are no universally accepted, comprehensive theories of how policy is made, or indeed how decisions are reached, in the public sector. The work that has been done does provide some assistance to the person who wants a better, although it will not by any means be complete, understanding of the process.

The organizational approach used by Taylor illustrates how a very complete picture of the process of decision making in one policy area can be obtained; the conflict resolution idea is significant because it focuses attention on the fundamental process of government, that is the "resolving, through an endless series of compromises, the conflicting interests of those subject to its authority in such a way as to avoid the open use of force."[13]

The muddling through theory explains and predicts a continuation of growth of government. Administrators by the nature of their training and positions do not, normally, seek a decrease in legislation or regulation as a solution to a problem; normally they opt for more. If there is a central theme of all explanations, particularly the incrementalist, it is that the system of decision making in government is structured in such a way that fashioning major policy change is almost impossible and that we should look, therefore, unless there are some dramatic changes in the structure of government, for an ever-increasing amount of activity by government in society.

Notes

[1] Adam Smith, *An Inquiry into the Nature and Causes of the Wealth of Nations* (New York: Modern Library, 1937), p. 423

[2] Joseph A. Schumpeter, *Can Capitalism Survive?* (New York: Harper Colophin Books, 1978), p. xii.

[3] For an excellent discussion of various theories see Peter Aucoin, "Public-Policy Theory and Analysis," in *Public Policy in Canada: Organization, Process, and Management*, edited by G. Bruce Doern and Peter Aucoin (Toronto: Macmillan, 1979). The position of the incrementalists, public choice, Marxists, and environmentalists are all carefully assessed. The *Eighth Annual Review* of the Economic Council of Canada is totally devoted to reviewing the process of decision making in government. For further analysis, see Richard Simeon, "Studying Public Policy," *Canadian Journal of Political Science* 9 (December 1976): 548–80.

[4] Malcolm Taylor, *Health Insurance and Canadian Public Policy* (McGill-Queen's University Press, 1978).

[5] David Easton, *A Framework for Political Analysis* (Englewood Cliffs, N.J.: Prentice-Hall, 1965).

[6] Taylor, *op. cit.*, p. xv.

[7] Economic Council of Canada, *Eighth Annual Review: Design for Decision-Making — An Application to Human Resources Policies* (Ottawa: Information Canada, 1971), p. 30.

[8] See Richard D. French, *How Ottawa Decides: Planning and Industrial Policy-Making 1968–1980* (Toronto: Canadian Institute for Economic Policy, 1980); Colin Campbell and George J. Szablowski, *The Superbureaucrats: Structure and Behaviour in Central Agencies* (Toronto: Macmillan, 1979).

[9] Douglas G. Hartle, "Techniques and Processes of Administration," *Canadian Public Administration* 19 (Spring 1976), pp. 24-29.

[10] Charles Lindblom, "The Science of 'Muddling Through'," *Public Administration Review* 19 (Spring 1959), p. 86.

[11] *Ibid.*, p. 86.

[12] *Ibid.*, p. 87.

[13] Douglas G. Hartle, *Public Policy Decision Making and Regulation* (Montreal: The Institute for Research on Public Policy, 1979), p. 34.

Bibliography

Ackerman, Robert W. "How Companies Respond to Social Demands." *Harvard Business Review* 51 (July-August 1973): 88–98.

Aitken, H.G.J. "Defensive Expansion: The State and Economic Growth in Canada." In *Approaches to Canadian Economic History*, edited by W.T. Easterbrook and M.H. Watkins, pp. 183–221. Toronto: McClelland and Stewart, 1967.

Aldag, Ramon J. and Jackson, Donald W. "Assessment of Attitudes Toward Social Responsibilities." *Journal of Business Administration* 8 (Spring 1977): 65–80.

Ansoff, H. Igor. "The Changing Shape of the Strategic Problem." In *Strategic Management: A New View of Business Policy and Planning*, edited by Dan E. Schendel and Charles W. Hofer, pp. 30–44. Boston: Little, Brown, 1979.

Archbold, W.D. "Business Council on National Issues: A New Factor in Business Communication." *The Canadian Business Review* 4 (Summer 1977): 13–15.

Aucoin, Peter. "Public-Policy Theory and Analysis." In *Public Policy in Canada: Organization, Process, and Management*, edited by G. Bruce Doern and Peter Aucoin, pp. 1– 26. Toronto: Macmillan, 1979.

Auld, D.A. *Issues in Government Expenditure Growth*. Montreal: C.D. Howe Research Institute, Canadian Economic Policy Committee, 1976.

Bell, Daniel. "The Corporation and Society in the 1970's." *The Public Interest* (Summer 1971): 5–32.

Beveridge, William H. *Full Employment in a Free Society*. New York: W.W. Norton, 1945.

Bird, Richard M. with Bucovetsky, R.W. and Foot, D.K. *The Growth of Public Employment in Canada*. Montreal: The Institute for Research on Public Policy, 1979.

Bok, Derek. *The President's Report 1977–78*. Cambridge: Harvard University, 1977.

Bothwell, Robert and Kilbourn, William. *C.D. Howe: A Biography*. Toronto: McClelland and Stewart, 1979.

Campbell, Colin and Szablowski, George J. *The Superbureaucrats: Structure and Behaviour in Central Agencies*. Toronto: Macmillan, 1979.

Canada. Auditor General. *Report of the Auditor General of Canada to the House of Commons for the Fiscal Year Ended March 31, 1976*. Ottawa: Minister of Supply and Services Canada, 1976.

Canada. Department of Industry, Trade and Commerce. *Small Business in Canada: A Statistical Profile*. Ottawa: The Department, 1979.

Canada. Parliament. House of Commons. *An Act to Register Lobbyists*. Bill C-255. Fourth Session, Thirtieth Parliament, October 1978.

Canada. Royal Commission on Corporate Concentration. *Report*. Ottawa: Minister of Supply and Services Canada, 1978.

Canada. Royal Commission on Financial Management and Accountability. *Final Report*. Ottawa: Minister of Supply and Services Canada, 1979.

Canada. Royal Commission on Financial Management and Accountability. *Progress Report*. Ottawa: Minister of Supply and Services Canada, 1977.

D'Aquino, Thomas D.; Doern, G. Bruce; and Blair, Cassandra. *Parliamentary Government in Canada: A Critical Assessment and Suggestions for Change*. A study prepared for the Business Council on National Issues. Ottawa: Intercounsel Limited, 1979.

Davis, Keith and Blomstron, Robert L. *Business, Society, and Environment: Social Power and Social Response*, 2d ed. New York: McGraw Hill, 1971.

Dimma, William A. "Government, Business, Labor: Some Future Directions." *Business Quarterly* 41 (Summer 1976): 37–49.

Drucker, Peter F. *The Age of Discontinuity*. New York: Harper and Row, 1969.

Drucker, Peter F. *Management: Tasks, Responsibilities, Practice*. New York: Harper and Row, 1974.

Economic Council of Canada. *Eighth Annual Review: Design for Decision-Making — An Application to Human Resources Policies*. Ottawa: Information Canada, 1971.

Economic Council of Canada. *First Annual Review: Economic Goals for Canada to 1970*. Ottawa: Queen's Printer, 1964.

Edmonds, J. Duncan. "The Public Affairs Function in Canadian Corporations." Ottawa: JDE Consulting Services, 1975.

French, Richard D. *How Ottawa Decides: Planning and Industrial Policy-Making 1968–1980*. Toronto: Canadian Institute for Economic Policy, 1980.

French, Richard D. "The Privy Council Office: Support for Cabinet Decision Making." In *The Canadian Political Process*, 3d ed., edited by Richard Schultz, Orest M. Kruhlak, and John C. Terry, pp. 363–94. Toronto: Holt, Rinehart and Winston, 1979.

Friedman, Milton. *Capitalism and Freedom*. Chicago: University of Chicago Press, 1962.

Friedman, Milton. *Essays in Positive Economics*. Chicago: University of Chicago Press, 1953.

Friedman, Milton. "The Social Responsibility of Business Is to Increase Its Profits." *The New York Times Magazine* (13 September 1970).

Galbraith, John Kenneth. *Economics and the Public Purpose*. Boston: Houghton, Mifflin, 1973.

The Gallup Report. Toronto: The Gallup Poll of Canada–The Canadian Institute of Public Opinion, 10 February 1979.

Godfrey, John M. "Introductory Remarks" for Panel on *How to Deal Effectively with Governments*. Montebello: Institute of Canadian Advertising, September 1972.

Hardin, Herschel. *A Nation Unaware: The Canadian Economic Culture*. Vancouver: J.J. Douglas, 1974.

Hartle, Douglas G. *The Draft Memorandum to Cabinet*. Toronto: Institute of Public Administration of Canada, 1976.

Hartle, Douglas G. *Public Policy Decision Making and Regulation*. Montreal: The Institute for Research on Public Policy, 1979.

Hartle, Douglas G. "Techniques and Processes of Administration," canadian Public Administration 19 (Spring 1976): 21–33.

Hayek, Frederick A. *The Road to Serfdom*. Chicago: University of Chicago Press, 1944.

Henning, Joel F. "Corporate Social Responsibility: Shell Game for the Seventies?" In *Corporate Power in America*, edited by Ralph Nader and Mark J. Green, pp. 151–70. New York: Grossman, 1973.

Institute for Public Involvement. *A Report on the Prospects for Increased Involvement of Business People in the Canadian Political System*. Toronto: Institute for Public Involvement, 1978.

Jackson, R.J. and Atkinson, M.M. "The Government's Legislative Programme and Its Linkage to Parliament." In *Apex of Power: The Prime Minister and Political Leadership in Canada*, 2d ed., edited by T. Hockin, pp. 237–46. Scarborough: Prentice-Hall, 1977.

Jacoby, N.H. "Capitalism and Contemporary Social Problems." *Sloan Management Review* 12 (Winter 1971): 33–43.

Jupp, Alex. "A Tyro MP Collides with 'the Process'." *Executive* 22 (May 1980): 46–48, 50.

Kierans, Eric. "The Corporate Challenge to Government." *The Walter L. Gordon Lecture Series 1976–77: The Role of Government in Canadian Society*. Toronto: The Canada Studies Foundation, 1977.

Kirby, M.J.L. and Kroeker, H.V. "The Politics of Crisis Management in Government: Does Planning Make Any Difference?" In *Studies on Crisis Management*, edited by C.F. Smart and W.T. Stanbury, pp. 179–95. Montreal: The Institute for Research on Public Policy, 1978.

Kniewasser, A. "How Do You Communicate with Government." Speech to the 68th Annual Convention of the Ontario Chamber of Commerce, Toronto, 13 May 1980.

Kniewasser, A. "Up Against Queen's Park." Speech to the University of Toronto, March 1980.

Lalonde, Marc. "The Changing Role of the Prime Minister's Office." *Canadian Public Administration* 14 (Winter 1971): 509–37.

Laundy, P. *Parliament's Role in the Control of Government Expenditures*. Ottawa: Research Branch, Parliamentary Library, 1977.

Lee, William M. "Business-Government — A Case for Involvement." Speech to the Board of Trade, Ottawa, October 1971.

Lee, William M. *A Profile of Executive Consultants Limited*. Ottawa Executive Consultants Ltd., 1980.

Lee, William M. Speech to the Toronto Ticker Club, 17 October 1975.

Lindblom, Charles E. "The Science of 'Muddling Through'." *Public Administration Review* 19 (Spring 1959): 79–88.

Litvak, Isaiah A. "The Ottawa Syndrome: Improving Business/Government Relations." *Business Quarterly* 44 (Summer 1979): 22–29.

Lovink, J.A.A. "Parliamentary Reform and Governmental Effectiveness in Canada." *Canadian Public Administration* 16 (Spring 1973): 35–54.

Macdonald, W.A. "Corporate Needs and Public Expectations." Speech to the Conference Board in Canada, Toronto, 6 March 1980.

MacIntosh, R.M. "The Role of Business in Public Policy." Remarks to the Institute of Management Consultants of Ontario, Toronto, 14 May 1979.

Mactaggart, R. Terrance; Kelly, Donald; Broadmore, Peter; and Preston, Lee E. *Corporate Social Performance in Canada*. Background study prepared for the Royal Commission on Corporate Concentration. Ottawa: Minister of Supply and Services Canada, 1977.

McGrath, Phyllis S. *Action Plans for Public Affairs*. Report No. 733. New York: Conference Board, 1977.

McKeough, W. Darcy. Remarks to The Young Presidents Organization, London, 6 May 1980.

McKichan, Alasdair J. "Comments" on W.T. Stanbury, "Lobbying and Interest Group Representation in the Legislative Process." In *The Legislative Process in Canada: The Need for Reform*, edited by W.A.W. Neilson and J.C. MacPherson, pp. 219–24. Montreal: The Institute for Research on Public Policy, 1978.

Meyer, Herbert E. "Business Wins One in Canada." *Fortune* (3 July 1978): 84–85.

Mill, John Stuart. "On Liberty." In *Utilitarianism, Liberty, and Representative Government* (New York: E.P. Dutton, 1951).

Monsen, B. Joseph. "Social Responsibility and the Corporation: Alternatives for the Future of Capitalism." *Journal of Economic Issues* 6 (March 1972): 125–41.

Neilson, W.A.W. and MacPherson, J.C., eds. *The Legislative Process in Canada: The Need for Reform*. Montreal: The Institute for Research on Public Policy, 1978.

Neville, W.H. *The Individual, the Political Party and Interest Groups in Modern Political Democracy*. Ottawa: Office of the Leader of the Opposition, 1976.

Peterson, Rein. *Small Business: Building a Balanced Economy*. Erin: Porcépic Press, 1977.

Pitfield, Michael. "The Shape of Government in the 1980s: Techniques and Instruments for Policy Formulation at the Federal Level." *Canadian Public Administration* 19 (Spring 1976): 8–20.

Post, James. "The Corporation in the Public Policy Process — A View Toward the 1980s." *Sloan Management Review* 21 (Fall 1979): 45–52.

Presthus, Robert. *Elite Accommodation in Canadian Politics*. Toronto: Macmillan, 1973.

Presthus, Robert. "Evolution and Canadian Political Culture — The Politics of Accommodation." Paper prepared for the *Bi-Centennial Conference on Revolution and Evolution: The Impact of Revolutionary Experience in the United States Compared to the Development of Canada Solely by Evolution*. North Carolina: Duke University, Canadian Studies Center, October 1976.

Presthus, Robert. "Interest Groups and the Canadian Parliament: Activities, Interaction, Legitimacy, and Influence." *Canadian Journal of Political Science* 4 (December 1971): 444–60.

Preston, Lee E. "Corporation and Society: The Search for a Paradigm." *Journal of Economic Literature* 13 (June 1975): 434–54.

Pross, A. Paul. "Canadian Pressure Groups in the 1970s: Their Role and Their Relations with the Public Service." *Canadian Public Administration* 18 (Spring 1975): 121–36.

Reid, John M. "The Backbencher and the Discharge of Legislative Responsibilities." In *The Legislative Process in Canada: The Need for Reform*, edited by W.A.W. Neilson and J.C. MacPherson, pp. 139–45. Montreal: The Institute for Research on Public Policy, 1978.

Reuber, Grant L. *Canada's Political Economy: Current Issues*. Toronto: McGraw-Hill Ryerson, 1980.

Robertson, Gordon. "The Changing Role of the Privy Council Office." *Canadian Public Administration* 14 (Winter 1971): 487–508.

Roman, Andrew. "Comments" on W.T. Stanbury, "Lobbying and Interest Group Representation in the Legislative Process." In *The Legislative Process in Canada: The Need for Reform*, edited by W.A.W. Neilson and J.C. MacPherson, pp. 208–17. Montreal: The Institute for Research on Public Policy, 1978.

Rush, Michael. "The Development of the Committee System in the Canadian House of Commons — Diagnosis and Revitalization." *The Parliamentarian* 55 (April 1974): 86–94.

Rush, Michael. "The Development of the Committee System in the Canadian House of Commons — Reassessment and Reform." *The Parliamentarian* 55 (July 1974): 149–58.

Schumpeter, Joseph A. *Can Capitalism Survive?* New York: Harper Colophin, 1978.

Schwindt, Richard. "Business and Society: A Review of the Work of the Royal Commission." In *Perspectives on the Royal Commission on Corporate Concentration*, edited by P.K. Gorecki and W.T. Stanbury, pp. 271–301. Montreal: The Institute for Research on Public Policy, 1979.

Silk, Leonard. *The Economists*. New York: Basic Books, 1976.

Silk, Leonard and Vogel, David. *Ethics and Profits: The Crisis of Confidence in American Business*. New York: Simon and Schuster, 1978.

Simeon, Richard. "Studying Public Policy." *Canadian Journal of Political Science* 9 (December 1976): 548–80.

Simon, William E. *A Time for Truth*. New York: McGraw-Hill, 1978.

Smith, Adam. *An Inquiry into the Nature and Causes of the Wealth of Nations*. New York: Modern Library, 1937.

Stanfield, Robert L. "The Present State of the Legislative Process in Canada: Myths and Realities." In *The Legislative Process in Canada: The Need for Reform*, edited by W.A.W. Neilson and J.C. MacPherson, pp. 39–50. Montreal: The Institute for Research on Public Policy, 1978.

Stevens, Robert. "Lobbyists a Big Cog in Ottawa Economy." *The Ottawa Journal* (8 May, 1980).

Stigler, George J. *Production and Distribution Theories*. New York: Macmillan, 1941.

Taylor, Malcolm. *Health Insurance and Canadian Public Policy*. Montreal: McGill-Queen's University Press, 1978.

Thain, Donald H. "The Mistakes of Business in Dealing with Politics and Government." *Business Quarterly* 44 (Autumn 1979): 46–54.

Thain, Donald H. and Baetz, Mark. "Increasing Trouble Ahead for Business-Government Relations in Canada?" *Business Quarterly* 44 (Summer 1979): 56–65.

Thomas, Paul G. "Comments" on J.M. Reid, "The Backbencher and the Discharge of Legislative Responsibilities." In *The Legislative Process in Canada: The Need for Reform*, edited by W.A.W. Neilson and J.C. MacPherson, pp. 154–63. Montreal: The Institute for Research on Public Policy, 1978.

Yankelovich, I.D. "Social Values." In the William Elliott Lectures as quoted in M.D. Richards, *Organizational Goal Structures*. St. Paul: West Publishing, 1978.

The Members of the Institute

Institute Management

Gordon Robertson	President
Louis Vagianos	Executive Director
Raymond Breton	Director, Ethnic and Cultural Diversity Program
John M. Curtis	Director, International Economics Program
Rowland J. Harrison	Director, Natural Resources Program
Ian McAllister	Director, Regional Employment Opportunities Program
William T. Stanbury	Director, Regulation and Government Intervention Program
Zavis P. Zeman	Director, Technology and Society Program
Donald Wilson	Director, Conference and Seminars Program
Dana Phillip Doiron	Director, Communications Services
Ann C. McCoomb	Associate Director, Communications Services
Tom Kent	Editor, *Policy Options Politiques*

The Institute for Research on Public Policy

Publications Available*
November 1981

Books

Leroy O. Stone &
Claude Marceau
Canadian Population Trends and Public Policy Through the 1980s. 1977 $4.00

Raymond Breton
The Canadian Condition: A Guide to Research in Public Policy. 1977 $2.95

Raymond Breton
Une orientation de la recherche politique dans le contexte canadien. 1978 $2.95

J.W. Rowley &
W.T. Stanbury, eds.
Competition Policy in Canada: Stage II, Bill C-13. 1978 $12.95

C.F. Smart &
W.T. Stanbury, eds.
Studies on Crisis Management. 1978 $9.95

W.T. Stanbury, ed.
Studies on Regulation in Canada. 1978 $9.95

Michael Hudson
Canada in the New Monetary Order: Borrow? Devalue? Restructure! 1978 $6.95

W.A.W. Neilson &
J.C. MacPherson, eds.
The Legislative Process in Canada: The Need for Reform. 1978 $12.95

David K. Foot, ed.
Public Employment and Compensation in Canada: Myths and Realities. 1978 $10.95

W.E. Cundiff &
Mado Reid, eds.
Issues in Canada/U.S. Transborder Computer Data Flows. 1979 $6.50

David K. Foot
Public Employment in Canada: Statistical Series. 1979 $15.00

Meyer W. Bucovetsky, ed.
Studies on Public Employment and Compensation in Canada. 1979 $14.95

Richard French &
André Béliveau
The RCMP and the Management of National Security. 1979 $6.95

---

* Order Address: The Institute for Research on Public Policy
P.O. Box 9300, Station "A"
TORONTO, Ontario
M5W 2C7

Richard French &   *La GRC et la gestion de la sécurité nationale*. 1979
André Béliveau $6.95

Leroy O. Stone &   *Future Income Prospects for Canada's Senior*
Michael J. MacLean   *Citizens*. 1979 $7.95

Richard Bird (in collaboration   *The Growth of Public Employment in Canada*. 1979
with Bucovetsky & Foot) $12.95

G. Bruce Doern &   *The Public Evaluation of Government Spending*.
Allan M. Maslove, eds.   1979 $10.95

Richard Price, ed.   *The Spirit of the Alberta Indian Treaties*. 1979
                           $8.95

Richard J. Schultz   *Federalism and the Regulatory Process*. 1979
                           $1.50

Richard J. Schultz   *Le fédéralisme et le processus de réglementation*.
                           1979 $1.50

Lionel D. Feldman &   *Bargaining for Cities. Municipalities and*
Katherine A. Graham   *Intergovernmental Relations: An Assessment*. 1979
                           $10.95

Elliot J. Feldman &   *The Future of North America: Canada, the United*
Neil Nevitte, eds.   *States, and Quebec Nationalism*. 1979 $7.95

Maximo Halty-Carrere   *Technological Development Strategies for*
                           Developing Countries. 1979 $12.95

G.B. Reschenthaler   *Occupational Health and Safety in Canada: The*
                           Economics and Three Case Studies. 1979 $5.00

David R. Protheroe   *Imports and Politics: Trade Decision-Making in*
                           Canada, 1968–1979. 1980 $8.95

G. Bruce Doern   *Government Intervention in the Canadian Nuclear*
                           Industry. 1980 $8.95

G. Bruce Doern &   *Canadian Nuclear Policies*. 1980 $14.95
R.W. Morrison, eds.

W.T. Stanbury, ed.   *Government Regulation: Scope, Growth, Process*.
                           1980 $10.95

Yoshi Tsurumi with   *Sogoshosha: Engines of Export-Based Growth*.
Rebecca R. Tsurumi   1980 $8.95

Allan M. Maslove & Gene Swimmer	*Wage Controls in Canada, 1975 – 78: A Study in Public Decision Making.* 1980 $11.95
T. Gregory Kane	*Consumers and the Regulators: Intervention in the Federal Regulatory Process.* 1980 $10.95
Albert Breton & Anthony Scott	*The Design of Federations.* 1980 $6.95
A.R. Bailey & D.G. Hull	*The Way Out: A More Revenue-Dependent Public Sector and How It Might Revitalize the Process of Governing.* 1980 $6.95
Réjean Lachapelle & Jacques Henripin	*La situation démolinguistique au Canada: évolution passée et prospective.* 1980 $24.95
Raymond Breton, Jeffrey G. Reitz & Victor F. Valentine	*Cultural Boundaries and the Cohesion of Canada.* 1980 $18.95
David R. Harvey	*Christmas Turkey or Prairie Vulture? An Economic Analysis of the Crow's Nest Pass Grain Rates.* 1980 $10.95
Stuart McFadyen, Colin Hoskins & David Gillen	*Canadian Broadcasting: Market Structure and Economic Performance.* 1980 $15.95
Richard M. Bird	*Taxing Corporations.* 1980 $6.95
Albert Breton & Raymond Breton	*Why Disunity? An Analysis of Linguistic and Regional Cleavages in Canada.* 1980 $6.95
Leroy O. Stone & Susan Fletcher	*A Profile of Canada's Older Population.* 1980 $7.95
Peter N. Nemetz, ed.	*Resource Policy: International Perspectives.* 1980 $18.95
Keith A.J. Hay, ed.	*Canadian Perspectives on Economic Relations with Japan.* 1980 $18.95
Raymond Breton & Gail Grant	*La langue de travail au Québec: synthèse de la recherche sur la rencontre de deux langues.* 1981 $10.95
Diane Vanasse	*L'évolution de la population scolaire du Québec.* 1981 $12.95

Raymond Breton,   *Les frontières culturelles et la cohésion du Canada.*
Jeffrey G. Reitz &   1981 $18.95
Victor F. Valentine

David M. Cameron, ed.   *Regionalism and Supranationalism: Challenges
                           and Alternatives to the Nation-State in Canada and
                           Europe.* 1981 $9.95

Peter Aucoin, ed.   *The Politics and Management of Restraint in
                           Government.* 1981 $17.95

H.V. Kroeker, ed.   *Sovereign People or Sovereign Governments.*
                           1981 $12.95

Heather Menzies   *Women and the Chip.* 1981 $6.95

Nicole S. Morgan   *Nowhere to Go? Consequences of the Demographic
                           Imbalance in Decision-Making Groups of the
                           Federal Public Service.* 1981 $8.95

Nicole S. Morgan   *Où aller? Les conséquences prévisibles des
                           déséquilibres démographiques chez les groupes de
                           décision de la fonction publique fédérale.*
                           1981 $8.95

Peter N. Nemetz, ed.   *Energy Crisis: Policy Response*, 1981 $10.95

Allan Tupper &   *Public Corporations and Public Policy in Canada.*
G. Bruce Doern, eds.   1981 $16.95

James Gillies   *Where Business Fails.* 1981 $9.95

Occasional Papers

W.E. Cundiff   *Nodule Shock? Seabed Mining and the Future of the
(No. 1)   Canadian Nickel Industry.* 1978 $3.00

IRPP/Brookings   *Conference on Canadian-U.S. Economic Relations.*
(No. 2)   1978 $3.00

Robert A. Russel   *The Electronic Briefcase: The Office of the Future.*
(No. 3)   1978 $3.00

C.C. Gotlieb   *Computers in the Home: What They Can Do for
(No. 4)   Us—And to Us.* 1978 $3.00

Raymond Breton &   *Urban Institutions and People of Indian Ancestry.*
Gail Grant Akian   1978 $3.00
(No. 5)

K.A. Hay
(No. 6)

Friends or Acquaintances? Canada as a Resource Supplier to the Japanese Economy. 1979 $3.00

T. Atkinson
(No. 7)

Trends in Life Satisfaction. 1979 $3.00

Fred Thompson &
W.T. Stanbury
(No. 9)

The Political Economy of Interest Groups in the Legislative Process in Canada. 1979 $3.00

Pierre Sormany
(No. 11)

Les micro-esclaves: vers une bio-industrie canadienne. 1979 $3.00

David Hoffman &
Zavis P. Zeman, eds.
(No. 13)

The Dynamics of the Technological Leadership of the World. 1980 $3.00

Russell Wilkins
(No. 13*a*)

Health Status in Canada, 1926–1976. 1980 $3.00

Russell Wilkins
(No. 13*b*)

L'état de santé au Canada, 1926–1976. 1980 $3.00

P. Pergler
(No. 14)

The Automated Citizen: Social and Political Impact of Interactive Broadcasting. 1980 $4.95

Zavis P. Zeman
(No. 15)

Men with the Yen. 1980 $5.95

Donald G. Cartwright
(No. 16)

Official Language Populations in Canada: Patterns and Contacts. 1980 $4.95

Report
Dhiru Patel

Dealing With Interracial Conflict: Policy Alternatives. 1980 $5.95

Working Papers (No Charge)**
W.E. Cundiff
(No. 1)

Issues in Canada/U.S. Transborder Computer Data Flows. 1978 (Out of print; in IRPP book of same title.)

** Order Working Papers from
The Institute for Research on Public Policy
P.O. Box 3670
Halifax South
Halifax, Nova Scotia
B3J 3K6

John Cornwall   *Industrial Investment and Canadian Economic*
(No. 2)   *Growth: Some Scenarios for the Eighties*. 1978

Russell Wilkins   *L'espérance de vie par quartier à Montréal, 1976:*
(No. 3)   *un indicateur social pour la planification*. 1979

F.J. Fletcher &   *Canadian Attitude Trends, 1960–1978*. 1979
R.J. Drummond
(No. 4)